Informality and the Playing Field in Vietnam's Business Sector

Informality and the Playing Field in Vietnam's Business Sector

Stoyan Tenev,
Amanda Carlier,
Omar Chaudry, and
Quynh-Trang Nguyen

IFC, World Bank, and MPDF
WASHINGTON, D.C.

2003

ISBN 0-8213-5647-X

Contents

Foreword

Vietnam made remarkable progress in the 1990s. The economy doubled, and poverty was cut in half. These achievements reflect continued progress in market reforms and in integrating with the world economy. They are, however, but the first steps across a challenging terrain. To create jobs for the unemployed, underemployed, and new additions to the work force, Vietnam will have to double the economy again by the end of the decade.

Keeping economic growth on track will require improvements in the business environment. It will need more supportive policies for private initiatives, for deepening banking and financial sector reforms, and for developing the legal system. Especially important is the small- and medium-scale private sector for generating jobs and translating savings into investment. Increasingly, growth opportunities for Vietnam will be linked with participation in the world economy. Vietnamese firms need to be prepared to respond effectively to the opportunities and challenges of globalization.

Recognizing that development and growth require certain enabling conditions, this study explores the business environment in Vietnam from the perspective of supporting economic growth. It focuses on informality and the evenness of the playing field in Vietnam's business sector. The study is based on findings from a survey of private and state-owned enterprises (SOEs) in 11 Vietnamese cities. It reflects the views of Vietnamese entrepreneurs on the business environment and incorporates the feedback from discussions with policy makers, financiers, and representatives of international organizations.

The study provides evidence of the significant improvements that have taken place in the Vietnamese business environment. It also identifies areas where policy actions can help to create a more transparent, predictable legal and regulatory framework and even the playing field for the private domestic-owned companies, the state-owned enterprises, and the foreign-invested companies. We hope that this study will provide all those with an interest in the development of the Vietnamese economy with new insights into its status and new ideas for ways to support and participate in its future growth.

JAVED HAMID, *Director*
East Asia and Pacific, IFC

HAROLD ROSEN, *Director*
Small and Medium Enterprise Department, World Bank Group

KLAUS ROHLAND, *Director for Vietnam*
World Bank

Acknowledgments

This study is a joint product of IFC's East Asia and Pacific Department, the Mekong Private Sector Development Facility, and the World Bank's Private Sector Development Unit. Mario Fischel, Javed Hamid, Deepak Khanna, Homi Kharas, Klaus Rohland, and Andrew Steer provided guidance and support. We acknowledge gratefully the support of the Australian Agency for International Development.

The cooperation of the Ministry of Planning and Investment in Vietnam and its local offices during the fieldwork in the survey locations was invaluable. Dr. Dinh Van An, president of the Central Institute for Economic Management, provided assistance and encouragement. We thank Tran Kim Hao, Vo Tri Thanh, and other colleagues at the institute for their contribution to the project. Special thanks go to Dinh Hien Minh for her enormous efforts in data entry and processing work.

Ligang Song of the Asia Pacific School of Economics and Management of the Australian National University provided excellent leadership in conducting the survey work and in preparing the technical report on the survey results. We are thankful to Quang Hong Doan from the National Centre for Development Studies at the university for his contribution to the survey work and the technical report and to Rana Ganguly for his administrative support.

Edmund Malesky and Vo Chau Giang provided background notes on local governments and business services. We are grateful to Mr. Le Dang Doanh of the Central Institute for Economic Management and Mme. Pham Chi Lan of the Vietnam Chamber of Commerce and Industry for their invaluable guidance and insights. Arvind Gupta, Liesbet Steer, and Markus Taussig provided useful comments and advice.

Simeon Djankov, David Dollar, Mary Hallward-Driemeier, and Frank Lysy from the World Bank Group were peer reviewers. Useful comments were received from Soren Davidsen, Daniel Musson,

Rakesh Nangia, Martin Rama, James Seward, Andy Stone, and Viet Dinh Tuan. Ting Lu provided valuable assistance. Udayan Wagle, Mariko Higashi, and Fred Wright supported the work through funding from the IFC Trust Funds. Vicky Macintyre edited the volume, and Dana Lane organized the production. Other assistance was provided by Thuy Huong Phan.

Abbreviations and Acronyms

APSEM	Asia Pacific School of Economics and Management
ASEAN	Association of Southeast Asian Nations
CEE	Central and Eastern Europe
CEO	Chief executive officer
CIEM	Central Institute of Economic Management
CIS	Commonwealth of Independent States
CLUR	Certificate of land-use rights
DPI	Department of Planning and Investment
FDI	Foreign direct investment
FIE	Foreign-invested enterprise
GDLA	General Department for Land Administration
GDP	Gross domestic product
GSO	General Statistical Office
HCMC	Ho Chi Minh City
IFC	International Finance Corporation
IT	Information technology
JSB	Joint-stock bank
LLC	Limited liability company
MENA	Middle East and North Africa region
MPDF	Mekong Private Sector Development Facility
MPI	Ministry of Planning and Investment (Vietnam)
NPL	Nonperforming loan
ODA	Official Development Assistance
OECD	Organization for Economic Cooperation and Development
OSS	One-stop shop
PJSB	Private joint-stock bank

SOCB	State-owned commercial bank
SOE	State-owned enterprise
SME	Small and medium enterprise
VAT	Value-added tax
VBF	Vietnamese Business Forum
VCCI	Vietnam Chamber of Commerce and Industry
VSS	Vietnam Social Security

Overview

Vietnam's remarkable growth performance in recent years has been accompanied by a significant increase in the size of the unofficial economy. It is estimated that for every dollar of official GDP, half a dollar goes unrecorded. Three out of every four real estate transactions are believed to take place in the unofficial market. For each company listed on the official stock exchange, there are about 30 companies trading on the informal stock market. Is this growth pattern sustainable? Can Vietnam achieve its ambitious goals by growing a largely informal economy?

A high level of informality is the work of structural factors that can hinder Vietnam's developmental objectives. Everywhere, widespread informality points to an environment of excessive regulation and ineffective enforcement. It means that rules and regulations are not binding and are therefore ineffective as tools of government policy.

If rules and regulations are well structured, informality undermines them by offering unfair advantage to noncompliant firms, thereby distorting the allocation of resources. Alternatively, if rules and regulations are unfair or if their application is biased, informality may be an efficient response by disadvantaged firms trying to even out the playing field.

Under either scenario, informality can be very costly. For example, firms operating at high levels of informality find it difficult to form partnerships and trade across national boundaries. Increasingly, growth opportunities for Vietnam will be linked with globalization. Formality will influence the extent to which otherwise competitive Vietnamese enterprises will be able to respond successfully to the opportunities and challenges of globalization.

This study focuses on informality and unevenness in Vietnam's business environment. It draws its findings from a survey of private and state-owned enterprises (SOEs) in 11 Vietnamese provinces. For the purposes of this study, informality refers to officially unrecorded activities of registered firms including activities that are to various degrees not in accordance with applicable regulations. Unregistered firms are not covered.

Informality: Patterns and Impact

This study explores three main questions. Are there any patterns of informality with respect to firm characteristics such as size and ownership? What are some of the factors contributing to higher informality among Vietnamese firms? Is informality costly? This section summarizes some of the main findings.

Excessive Administrative Burden Encourages Informality. Local governments can contribute to informality through excessive regulations and cumbersome administrative procedures. In the cities surveyed, informality increases in proportion to the time that enterprises spend dealing with regulatory requirements. For example, a two-day increase in the city average of management time spent dealing with regulations is associated with a one-point reduction in the percentage of workers with formal contracts.

Regulations and their applications often tend to encourage informality by penalizing success, growth, and visibility. For example, punitive taxes are imposed on returns in excess of 20 percent. At the same time, larger, faster-growing, and more licensed companies tend to be inspected more often. Tax inspections, in particular, show a strong and significant positive correlation with a firm's growth rate.

Uneven Playing Field Is Fertile Ground for Informality. Informality thrives in Vietnam in part because businesses of different ownership types and sizes are treated unequally. Private and smaller enterprises face more difficulties in accessing bank financing, land, and other critical resources. Administrative burdens are also uneven. Private companies tend to spend on average 9 days more of management time in dealing with regulations than state-owned companies do. The difference increases significantly to about 26 days when controlling for size, informality, performance, and export orientations. Private enterprises also receive inspectors on their premises more often. Yet they tend to be more informal than state-owned enterprises. Size, too, has bearing on informality: the smaller the enterprise, the more informal it is likely to be.

Informality Is Costly. Informality is not associated with reduced administrative burdens for firms. On the contrary, more informal companies tend to spend more managerial time "dealing" with regulatory requirements and pay a higher percentage of their total revenues in bribes. A 20 percent reduction in the share of the transactions going through banks, for example, is associated with a 50 percent increase in the share of revenues paid in unofficial payments. There are also indirect costs of informal business. Companies have reduced ability to enter into formal contracts and to access business services. The indirect costs of informality tend to be particularly important when it comes to interacting with foreign parties. Companies that rely less on the banking system to carry transactions, for example, tend to be less successful exporters.

Uneven Playing Field Leads to Misallocation of Resources. Different rules govern access to resources such as finance and land for different types of enterprises. Profitability and size, for example, are positively associated with access to bank loans for private enterprises but are unimportant in the case of state-owned enterprises. Yet state ownership is associated with an increase in the share of bank loans in total financing by 11 percent when controlling for size, by 18 percent when controlling for profitability, by 16 percent when controlling for possession of Certificates of Land Use Rights, and by 14 percent when controlling for all of these factors. In the case of land, many private enterprises have to wait for years to get the land they need to execute investment plans. At the same time, state enterprises typically have land in excess of their immediate and future needs.

Thus land and money do not flow to the entrepreneurs that can put these resources into their most productive uses. Private enterprises in our sample tend to have a better financial and growth performance than state-owned enterprises. Their employment growth and return on assets, however, show a declining trend in the wake of the rapid growth of new registrations and increased competition in the private sector. Although this pattern is common in successful transition economies, it underscores the need for rapid improvements in the investment climate to sustain the process of robust business creation.

Implications for Policy

Greater formality carries significant social benefits, which can be achieved by reducing excessive regulatory burdens, making laws and regulations more reasonable and hence more enforceable, and leveling the playing field.

Making Rules More Reasonable. Laws and regulations that run against the interests of almost everybody in society not only are difficult to enforce but may erode the legitimacy of the government. The current regulatory framework in Vietnam offers examples of rules that run against the logic of normal market practices. Business success in the form of higher returns is taxed punitively. Expenditures that are particularly important for creating and exploiting market opportunities, such as marketing expenses, are not fully tax exempt. These measures encourage informality and penalize growth. Administrative biases against success need to be abolished.

Equally daunting to businesses is the approval and licensing spirit that still permeates many laws and regulations. The perceived need to have laws provide for every eventuality not only adds to the complexity of implementing regulations but increases the discretion of government officials. The practice of using rigid forms for important business transactions such as labor contracts and the leasing of land-use rights reflects a desire by the state to manage and control private transactions. The shift from concessionary (known as asking-giving in Vietnam) to normative regulations could bring significant benefits, as demonstrated by the passage and implementation of the Enterprise Law, and should be extended to other areas.

Strengthening Enforcement Capacity and Bureaucratic Accountability. In Vietnam's present administrative system, many government agencies that interact with the business community have overlapping responsibilities and lack clear accountability. As a result, administrative decision making is often slow. As roles and responsibilities within the bureaucracy become more clearly delineated, government-business interactions should improve. At the provincial level there is much to gain from one-stop delivery of government services. To increase the government's accountability in its interactions with business, entrepreneurs need to have better access to the administrative court system. In particular, the filing process needs to be simplified and made less costly.

Using Indirect Mechanisms to Enforce Regulations. To economize on resources, the government should rely more on indirect forms of control in enforcing complex regulations. Although individual firms may be tempted to skirt regulations, enforcement is often in the collective interest of entrepreneurs. As instruments of collective actions, business associations can internalize the public benefits associated with regulations and taxation and thus can play an important role in fostering formality. To do so, however, they need to be financially independent from the government. To this end, they should be given standard tax exemptions on income from core activities and tax deductions for dues paid by members. They should also be allowed to provide a broader range of business services, such as trade and investment promotion, both of which are mainly under the aegis of state agencies at present. In addition, the government should authorize business associations to carry out some tasks and projects of a public service nature such as providing business support services. Business associations, however, should not be allowed to become instruments in the hands of incumbents for restricting market access.

Reforming SOEs to Level the Playing Field. Although Vietnam has made significant progress toward leveling the playing field, there are still systematic biases in the business environment against private enterprises. These biases can be eliminated through deeper reform of the state sector and improved access to capital and land for private firms. Circumstances in Vietnam are particularly complex because the authorities intend to retain a sizable number of enterprises under state control; yet, in the view of the private sector, state ownership encourages government intervention in the economy. To create a more level playing field for state-owned and private enterprises, enterprise reform should include measures to corporatize state enterprises, diversify ownership, and manage state assets efficiently. Such reforms will in turn ensure that equitized companies will not experience problems as soon as they sever their links with the government.

Addressing Demand- and Supply-Side Issues to Improve Access to Finance. Corporatization and equitization will create a more level playing field with respect to access to financing. At present, state-owned enterprises continue to enjoy preferential access to financing, while the private sector, particularly its small and medium enterprises, is underserved by the banking sector. A variety of reasons contribute to this state of affairs, on both the demand and the supply side of the credit market.

On the supply side, a bank may be reluctant to lend to private companies that have no government backing because it may lack the training and experience to conduct a sound risk appraisal. With the recent removal of restrictions on interest rates, banks are now able to price the risk into their loans if they can assess the risk accurately. Hence banks need to strengthen their risk-assessment skills and be able to base loans not only on collateral but also on the intrinsic merits of a project.

On the demand side, private enterprises are often reluctant to seek bank credit because their business activities must meet higher standards of transparency. Domestic private companies can and should take the necessary steps to meet these criteria. To further improve their access to credit and their ability to grow, domestic private firms need to formalize their structures and operations and upgrade their management skills. In this way, they will not only gain greater access to outside sources of finance but also increase their global competitiveness. Enterprises will be reluctant to take such steps, however, unless they have confidence in the system and know that such action will be rewarded with even greater political acceptance, less bureaucratic interference, and more access to finance.

Accessing Land on More Equal Basis. The main problem private firms face in obtaining bank loans is insufficient collateral, which to a large extent relates to the inefficient system of land administration and prohibitively high cost of land-use rights. Because the system discriminates between domestic and foreign users of land, domestic enterprises find it difficult to partner with foreign parties or to obtain financing from offshore financial institutions. Under the current legal and regulatory framework, with its different regimes for residential and commercial land, the playing field is uneven in certain sectors, and businesses are reluctant to convert land from personal to firm ownership. The transaction costs associated with conversion to commercial use should be reduced so that enterprises can adopt the legal form most suitable for their growth plans and strategy.

Market-friendly Regulations

Private sector growth will be key to maintaining the dynamism of the Vietnamese economy and allowing the country to achieve its development objectives. Above all, private enterprises need space to grow. Regulations that run counter to the logic of normal market practices, that give entrepreneurs few opportunities to enter into contractual relationships, or that penalize them for market success are bound to be circumvented, at significant social cost. By contrast, laws and regulations that are in harmony with market forces will be easier to implement, and their implementation will be supported by the same market forces they are designed to protect. Adapting laws and regulations to the needs of the marketplace will not be enough, however. Incentives inside the bureaucracy need to be aligned with development. A government that is committed to development will find it beneficial to support the growth of the private sector.

1
Introduction

The development story in Vietnam in recent years has been one of remarkable progress (Dollar 2002). Over the 1990s, the economy doubled and the incidence of poverty declined by half. Although these are indeed notable achievements, they are but the first steps across a difficult terrain. About 30 million people, or more than a third of the total population, continue to live in poverty, and 25 million, or about 60 percent of the labor force, are either underemployed or unemployed. To create jobs for the unemployed, underemployed, and new additions to the work force, Vietnam will have to double the economy again by the end of the decade, but this cannot happen unless both the level and the quality of investment increase substantially. According to World Bank estimates, average total investment must reach 30 percent of gross domestic product (GDP) by 2010, which represents a 5 percent increase over the 1990s, while average productivity will have to be about 40 percent higher (World Bank 2001). To achieve these objectives, Vietnam needs to encourage the private sector to contribute more to economic growth. This will require significant improvements in its business environment.

The Private Sector and Vietnam's Development Challenges

The government of Vietnam has already launched a reform program that is helping to restrain the growth of investment in the state sector. Also significant, foreign direct investment (FDI) has stabilized at around $1 billion a year and may increase if Vietnam's investment environment begins to compare more favorably with that of the countries of the Association of Southeast Asian Nations (ASEAN) and of China. The challenge will be to sustain FDI at levels achieved prior to the Asian crisis of 1997. Hence the onus will be on the domestic private sector not only to contribute the additional 5 percent of GDP in investment but also to compensate for the expected

1

decline in investment in state-owned enterprises (SOEs). The reallocation of investment resources from the state to the private sector should push productivity to levels that can help Vietnam reach its development objectives.

With the shift away from the state sector, the domestic private sector, mainly its small and medium enterprises (SMEs), will have to create most of the new jobs. In the SOE sector, currently employing about 1.7 million people, restructuring is expected to bring redundancies (Belser and Rama 2002). Although the foreign-invested enterprise sector (FIE) is an important source of high-paying jobs, close to 90 percent of the stock of foreign investment is in capital-intensive industries. Therefore most of the job creation will fall to the domestic private SMEs, which are generally more labor intensive and export oriented. Furthermore, the manufacturing output of private SMEs will have to grow by 18–25 percent a year to generate the number and types of jobs that the country needs (World Bank 2001).

How attainable are these objectives? Recent trends in private sector growth and investment are encouraging. The formal private sector has been expanding rapidly and in the past few years has emerged as the most dynamic component of the Vietnamese economy. Between January 2000 and December 2002 alone, Vietnam registered about 56,000 new private enterprises, which is more than the total number registered in the preceding decade. In the wake of this growth, gross capital formation jumped from 26 percent of GDP in 1999 to about 30 percent in 2001. Also impressive is the growth in private industrial output, which posted rates of 19.2 percent in 2000, 20.3 percent in 2001, and 19.3 percent in 2002. By contrast, SOEs and foreign-invested enterprises grew at 11.9 percent and 14.7 percent, respectively, over this period. Although at the lower end, this growth is within the 18–25 percent range that needs to be maintained to achieve Vietnam's development objectives. Another encouraging signal is emanating from private sector employment, where both new and existing companies added nearly 250,000 new wage jobs in 2001—a one-year increase of almost 45 percent.

All of these trends point to a significant shift in official attitudes toward private sector development, perhaps best reflected in the enactment of the Enterprise Law and the formal endorsement of the private sector following the Fifth Plenum of the Ninth Party Congress in March 2002. Despite all this progress and a certain degree of dynamism, however, Vietnam's formal domestic private sector remains small. As of 2002, it still accounted for less than 8 percent of total GDP, 6 percent of manufacturing output, and about 3 percent of total employment. Vietnam is perhaps the only transition economy in the world where the state sector's share in GDP and manufacturing has been increasing for most of the reform period. Hence it is not so surprising that the private sector's share in output has remained small and stagnant or that its impressive rates of job creation still cannot keep up with the growth of the overall work force. Clearly, Vietnam must do more to accelerate private sector growth if it is to attain its development objectives. The question is, what measures will move it in this direction?

Focus of the Study

To answer that question, one must first recognize that development and growth require a certain business environment. It must be supportive of the creation of new firms and the growth of micro, small, and medium enterprises into larger ones. This study explores the business environment in Vietnam from the perspective of supporting economic growth. It focuses on informality and the evenness of the playing field in Vietnam's business sector.

Informality refers to economic activities that are not in accord with prescribed regulations. The informal economy has been defined as "a process of income-generation characterized by one central feature: it is unregulated by the institutions of society, in a legal and social environment in which similar activities are regulated" (Portes, Castells, and Benton 1989:12). Informality does not, however, reflect a binary state of affairs, in which firms conduct all of their economic activities either within or outside the prescribed regulations. Rather, the typical pattern is an intermediate one, meaning a firm is compliant to varying degrees in the various areas of its business operations. This study is concerned with this intermediate form of informality.

Why does informality merit close attention? Informality is the product of government-business interactions in an environment of excessive regulations and ineffective enforcement. Regulations and laws are perhaps the most powerful tools that a developmental state possesses to bring about positive changes and reforms, but their effectiveness is severely curtailed in the presence of informality. When the business sector is highly informal, changes in economic laws and regulations will not lead to anticipated or intended changes in behavior and outcomes. In a word, informality weakens the government's arsenal of instruments for engineering improvements in the business environment. Therefore a top priority for the developmental state should be to reduce informality and make rules binding.

Informality has another important trait: it can alter the evenness of the playing field. If rules and regulations provide for a level playing field, informality gives an unfair competitive advantage to noncompliant firms. As such it distorts the allocation of resources and leads to economic inefficiency. Alternatively, if rules and regulations are unfair or their application biased, informality may be a socially efficient response by disadvantaged firms trying to even out the playing field. That is why it is essential to discuss informality and the evenness of the playing field in tandem.

Furthermore, informality greatly affects interactions between domestic and foreign companies. Enterprises operating at high levels of informality typically find it difficult to partner and trade across national boundaries. Vietnam is integrating into the global economy and preparing for membership in the World Trade Organization. Formality will influence the extent to which otherwise competitive Vietnamese enterprises will be able to respond successfully to the opportunities and challenges of globalization.

In light of all these factors, it is essential to consider the viewpoints of the local entrepreneurs. We asked the managers of private and state-owned enterprises in Vietnam to rank the severity of 33 obstacles in the areas of competition, access to resources, policy implementation, macroeconomic conditions, legal and regulatory framework, and infrastructure. From the top ten constraints identified by these managers (table 1.1), it is clear that the issues at the heart of this study are among the central concerns of Vietnamese entrepreneurs. They relate to government-business interactions, level of taxation, and the playing field in the areas of market competition and access to resources (for a detailed list of the constraints in Vietnam's business environment, see appendix table 1.3).

Empirical Approach

The study investigates the key aspects of the business environment in Vietnam through an empirical survey of private and state-owned enterprises. The survey instrument was designed by staff of the International Finance Corporation (IFC), the World Bank, and the Mekong

TABLE 1.1
MAIN CONSTRAINTS IN THE BUSINESS ENVIRONMENT
BY OWNERSHIP TYPE

SOEs		Private enterprises	
Constraint	Those with "major" or "severe" obstacle (%)	Constraint	Those with "major" or "severe" obstacle (%)
1. Unfair competition	64	1. Unfair competition	61
2. High tax rates	62	2. Weak demand	56
3. Uncertainty of policy	57	3. High tax rates	55
4. Weak demand	54	4. Access to financing	48
5. Inconsistency of policies	53	5. Inconsistency of policies	42
6. Bureaucracy	52	6. Uncertainty of policies	42
7. Macro-instability	47	7. Preferential treatment of SOEs	42
8. Lack of marketing knowledge	47	8. Bureaucracy	40
9. Managerial skills	42	9. Macro-instability	37
10. Cost of financing	35	10. Cost of financing	34

SOURCE: Author calculations based on survey data.

Private Sector Development Facility (MPDF). The survey was implemented by a research team comprising researchers from the Asia Pacific School of Economics and Management (APSEM) of the Australian National University and the Central Institute of Economic Management (CIEM) of Vietnam's Ministry of Planning and Investment (MPI). It was conducted in 11 provinces and cities of Vietnam: Hanoi, Ho Chi Minh City (HCMC), Hai Phong, Da Nang, Thua Thien Hue, Binh Duong, Dong Nai, Ha Tay, Long An, Nam Dinh, and Thanh Hoa.

Survey Instruments. Three types of instruments were used to survey businesses and local officials having direct interaction with or responsibilities related to the development of the economy: (1) questionnaires mailed out to enterprises before the fieldwork began; (2) interviews with the chief executive officers (CEOs) of a subset of the selected firms designed to gain deeper insights into issues facing the enterprise sector; and (3) interviews with government officials, representatives of relevant organizations, and commercial banks.

The questionnaires mailed to firms contained structured questions on factual aspects of a firm's operation and development. These questions were to be answered by persons designated by the CEOs, such as deputy managers or chief accountants. In total, questionnaires were sent to 3,900 randomly selected private enterprises and 400 SOEs before the research team conducted any interviews. The team received 746 completed questionnaires, 629 from private businesses and 117 from SOEs. Hence the overall response rate was 17 percent, and the rate for SOEs was 1.8 times that for private businesses. Some of the completed questionnaires were of poor quality and could not be coded and entered. Therefore the number of questionnaires processed is less than the actual number received.

Guided by a questionnaire containing both structured and open-ended questions, interviewers met with the CEOs of 295 firms (225 private enterprises and 70 SOEs). During the interviews, CEOs filled in the structured questions, and interviewers then posed the open-ended questions. These latter questions elicited CEOs' opinions on the most important and pressing issues their firms are facing and the changes needed to improve the business and policy environments in which they operate.

Before the start of the interviews, a training session was arranged to familiarize team members with the survey methodology, the questionnaires, and associated requirements. A pilot survey was then conducted in Hanoi and the feedback used to make final adjustments to the questionnaires, which were also based on suggestions from a number of international experts in Vietnam. Data processing was carried out by CIEM staff.

Sampling Strategy and Outcome. We adopted a stratified random sampling strategy to determine which businesses would receive questionnaires and which CEOs would be interviewed, choosing from a database constructed and maintained by the Central Institute of Economics and Management. Of the sample localities, only Ho Chi Minh City had an electronic database of all businesses located in the city. Another point to note is that the study focuses on domestic private and state-owned enterprises and excludes businesses with a significant foreign participation. Although Vietnam's domestic private sector encompasses business individuals and households registered by the law, the study also excludes business households, a very important component of the private sector, because of the difficulty of reaching them and obtaining accurate information on them.

Geographically, the distribution of the sampled firms was roughly similar to that of the country's population. Most of the contacted private firms were from the South, followed by the North and the Central regions. The response rate in the South was lower, however, which means that private enterprises in the North tend to be overrepresented and those in the South underrepresented in the sample. As for the SOE universe, it has fewer firms than the private sector and their geographical distribution is uneven, with Hanoi and HCMC dominating the picture. Instead of attempting to replicate the ownership structure of the economy in each province/city, we focused on the broader regional structure of the state-owned sector.

To ensure that our survey sample provided a representative picture of Vietnam's enterprise sector, we also tried to include areas at different levels of development. Hence they range from the economic powerhouses of HCMC, Hanoi, and Da Nang to provinces that have displayed slower economic development, such as Ha Tay, Nam Dinh (from the North), Thanh Hoa (from the Middle), and Long An (from the South). Owing to the disparity in economic development in those provinces, the number of businesses varies from province to province. In the less developed provinces of Thanh Hoa, Ha Tay, Nam Dinh, and Long An, the number of private businesses is small, and it was possible to reach all private enterprises.

The share of each type of legal form examined—sole proprietorship, partnership, limited liability company, and shareholding—was roughly the same as their respective share in the population of private enterprises. This was also the case for the state-owned enterprises, where we tried to mimic the structure in terms of central versus local control.

The sampling strategy was difficult to apply, however, because many local government agencies did not have the required data, or the contact information for private enterprises was inaccurate. Thus the enterprises covered in the survey tend to be concentrated in the part of the private sector that is easiest to identify and contact, namely, the larger, more mature private enterprises. These enterprises also have a stronger incentive to respond to the questionnaires.

As table 1.2 shows, on average the private enterprises in our sample tend to be significantly larger than the universe average. This

TABLE 1.2
SAMPLE VS. UNIVERSE CHARACTERISTICS

Characteristic	Private		SOE	
	Sample	Universe	Sample	Universe
Number of enterprises	629	29,519	117	4,740
Sectoral distribution (%)				
Industry	48	24	55	39
Trade	47	59	34	
Services	32	17	44	
Agriculture	2		3	
Regional distribution (%)				
North	43	22	52	33
Central	19	12	0	19
South	38	66	48	48
Number of employees				
Average	120	29	477	582
< 50 (%)	68		10	
50–99 (%)	12		16	
100–499 (%)	16		50	
> 500 (%)	4		24	
Legal form (%)				
Private	27	61		
Partnership	0	0		
Limited liability	67	37		
Shareholding	6	2		
SOE control (%)				
Central			48	37
Local			52	63
Equitized			7	7
Exporters (%)	34		48	
Direct exporters	20	24	42	54

SOURCE: World Bank staff estimates.

is driven by a few very large private enterprises, however. Almost 70 percent of our private enterprises have fewer than 50 employees. By contrast, on average the state-owned enterprises in our sample tend to be smaller than the population. Differences between our sample and the universe also exist in their sectoral distribution, geographical structure, and legal form. Industry, the North, and limited liability (central control for SOEs) tend to be overrepresented in our sample, while trade, the South, and sole proprietorship (local control for SOEs) are somewhat underrepresented.

Limitations of the Empirical Approach. An inherent feature of the survey approach is that the quality of the data is limited. To address this problem, we relied on both hard data and perception data. Managers were asked questions about quantifiable aspects of their firm's situation and behavior. They were also asked to rank the difficulties they face because of certain aspects of the business environment. Both types of data are prone to biases and imperfections.

For instance, a common problem with surveys is that some respondents may not report truthfully. In our case, biases could have been introduced when government officials were present at the interviews. Because some CEO interviews were conducted in the presence of Department of Planning and Investment (DPI) staff, the enterprises concerned may not have expressed their true opinions; hence some of the survey results could be inaccurate. However, local authorities were involved in relatively few interviews (about 12 enterprises). Furthermore, in Vietnam enterprise managers are usually not intimidated by government officials. On the contrary, they are anxious to voice their concerns to the authorities, which suggests that the opinions expressed in the survey may well reflect respondents' true views.

Another problem is selection bias. The provinces selected in this research project are not the least developed and most difficult business environments in Vietnam. Most respondent enterprises are relatively successful. By design, the survey does not capture failures. Therefore, the picture of business environments that emerges illustrates issues but is not representative of the whole experience of the enterprise sector in Vietnam. This is an important point that needs to be taken into account when analyzing and interpreting the survey results.

Perception data are particularly prone to biases, especially in relation to the ordering of the questions. That is why we tried to space out questions that are expected to show certain causal relationships and correlations. For example, we placed questions asking managers their perceptions about the fairness of competition a significant distance from questions about the type of competitors and their main advantages.

A more fundamental problem is that respondents may not put enough effort into answering the question. Long questionnaires are particularly prone to this problem, and it may affect the quality of the answers, especially to questions toward the end of the list. Therefore we kept our mail-out questionnaire fairly short. Although the CEO questionnaire was quite long, the problem there was mitigated by the live interaction between the interviewer and the respondent.

Still other limitations relate to the range of options offered to respondents and the norm they may infer from it. In our survey, they tended to congregate toward the middle of the range of answers. In view of these and other intrinsic problems of perception data, we place less weight on their absolute values and more weight on any systematic differences in perceptions among groups of enterprises, particularly private companies and SOEs. The assumption here is that the biases of perception data will affect different types of enterprise managers in the same way, so systematic within-sample differences are likely to reflect objective differences in the business environment.

Conclusion

We focus on a few characteristics of Vietnam's business environment, particularly informality and evenness of the playing field in the economy. A high degree of informality reduces the government's ability to apply regulatory tools to engineer improvements in the business environment. Therefore reducing informality and making rules binding should be a top priority for the developmental state. Informality can also affect the playing field, the allocation of resources, and overall economic efficiency. To explore these aspects of the business environment in Vietnam, we have collected data on the domestic enterprise sector through surveys and interviews with enterprise managers and government officials.

Our survey differs from other surveys done in Vietnam in several important repects. First, it is more comprehensive in its geographic coverage and sample size, covering 746 enterprises from 11 cities and provinces. Second, it contains both hard data and perception data derived from responses to two questionnaires: a short questionnaire mailed out to enterprises and a longer CEO questionnaire accompanied by an interview. Third, it covers both private and state-owned enterprises. Most previous surveys tended to focus on one or the other, thus presenting a partial picture of the business environment. By including both private and state-owned enterprises and focusing on systematic differences between the two, we have been able to over-come some of the limitations of perception data.

The following chapters summarize our survey results and con-clusions about business conditions in Vietnam. Chapter 2 presents an analysis of the data obtained on government-business interactions in Vietnam and the level of informality in the enterprise sector derived from the survey results; it also contains a review of the relevant liter-ature and some comments on other statistical surveys. Chapter 3 explores the playing field in areas that are particularly important for growth, such as access to financing, access to land, and product mar-ket competition. Chapter 4 offers suggestions for addressing some of the issues identified in the study in the hope that they and the other information in this volume will help Vietnam develop a business envi-ronment supportive of private sector growth.

Appendix

We asked managers to express their perceptions about the outstand-ing obstacles in the business environment in the areas of competition, access to resources, infrastructure, macro-conditions, and policy implementation (see appendix tables 1.3 and 1.4). Competition and general market conditions seem to be the most problematic areas for entrepreneurs, with unfair competition being the most severe obstacle. Access to resources is second in terms of severity of constraints. Here, the biggest constraint was said to be poor access to financing because of inadequate collateral. In the area of policy implementation, entre-preneurs complained most about bureaucracy, inconsistency, and uncertainty of policies. Laws and regulations are relatively low in the overall ranking. However, all respondents perceived tax regulations as a major obstacle. Interestingly, SOEs are more vocal than private entrepreneurs about difficulties in the business environment. In 27 of our 33 variables on various aspects of the business environment, the means for SOEs are higher than those for private enterprises, indicat-ing a higher level of perceived constraint. It is instructive to look at the areas where private entrepreneurs are more concerned than SOEs. These include reliability of electricity supply, access to land, weak demand, access to financing, preferential treatment of SOEs, and enforceability of laws and regulations.

TABLE 1.3
SEVERITY OF CONSTRAINTS IN THE BUSINESS ENVIRONMENT

Obstacles	Total	Private enterprises	SOEs
Infrastructure			
Electricity supply	1.73	1.76	1.67
Roads and ports	1.92	1.87	2.03
Communication	1.70	1.69	1.71
Land	1.99	2.02	1.93
Competition			
Market entry	2.24	2.22	2.28
Weak demand	2.57	2.58	2.56
Market information	2.27	2.26	2.28
Unfair competition	2.75	2.74	2.79
Distribution channels	2.01	1.89	2.29
Protectionism	1.80	1.71	2.00
Access to resources			
Skills of workers	2.08	1.98	2.32
Managerial talent	2.07	2.01	2.19
Technology	2.17	2.14	2.24
Marketing skills	2.14	2.02	2.42
Consulting services	1.81	1.77	1.92
Access to financing	2.37	2.43	2.21
Cost of financing	2.13	2.06	2.28
Laws and regulations			
Tax rates	2.53	2.46	2.67
Customs and trade	2.12	2.11	2.15
Business licensing and registration	1.44	1.36	1.63
Environment	1.61	1.57	1.71
Labor	1.77	1.76	1.79
Contract and property rights	1.51	1.42	1.71
Fire control and safety	1.58	1.50	1.75
Policy implementation			
Bureaucracy	2.37	2.30	2.53
Uncertainty of policies	2.43	2.34	2.63
Inconsistency of policies	2.37	2.31	2.47
Preferential treatment of SOEs	2.29	2.35	2.09
Enforceability of laws and regulations	1.70	1.74	1.61
Attitude of local governments	1.52	1.46	1.66
Macro-conditions			
Macroeconomic stability	2.19	2.15	2.26
Law and order	1.68	1.59	1.90
Corruption	1.93	1.89	2.02

NOTE: Indices are calculated by assigning a value of 4 if a constraint is perceived as severe, 3 if a constraint is perceived as major, 2 if minor, and 1 if no obstacle. The higher the number, the more severe the constraint.

TABLE 1.4
SUMMARY OF BUSINESS ENVIRONMENT CONSTRAINTS

Areas	Total	Private	SOEs
Competition	2.26	2.21	2.37
Access to resources	2.10	2.05	2.22
Policy implementation	2.05	2.02	2.11
Macro-conditions	1.93	1.88	2.06
Infrastructure	1.83	1.83	1.84
Laws and regulations	1.79	1.74	1.92

NOTE: Indices are calculated by assigning a value of 4 if a constraint is perceived as severe, 3 if a constraint is perceived as major, 2 if minor, and 1 if no obstacle. The higher the number, the more severe the constraint.
SOURCE: Author calculations based on survey data.

2
Government Interventions and Business Informality

Informality is a product of government-business interactions in an overregulated business environment with very high compliance costs and discretionary behavior by officials.[1] No businesses or individuals enjoy paying taxes or having to comply with various controls and regulations. Furthermore, the higher the overall level of compliance, the higher the temptation to evade compliance. At the same time, high levels of informality typically point to excessive taxes and regulations imposed by governments that lack the capability to enforce compliance. Hence a government can contribute to informality by unreasonable laws and regulations that impose very high compliance costs or by arbitrary and capricious applications of otherwise reasonable rules and regulations. Disentangling the "contributions" of the various interacting factors is difficult. This chapter looks at government business interactions in Vietnam from the perspective of their impact on business informality.

Level of Informal Business Activity in Vietnam

From sample surveys conducted in 1989, 1992, 1994, and 1996, the General Statistical Office (GSO) of Vietnam estimates that the GDP of the informal sector is more than half the size of the formal sector's GDP (GSO 2001).[2] Although it is home to all kinds of economic

---

1. It is important to emphasize that overregulation and discretionary behavior of officials are the problem, not informality itself, which can be viewed as a rational response in such a business environment.

2. In GSO's definition, informal activities include (1) household production in rural areas; (2) unregistered business activities in urban areas; (3) not reporting

14

activities, the informal sector derives its GDP mainly from secondary activity by agricultural households (24 percent of formal GDP), unreported trade and services in urban areas (10.5 percent), and unreported activities of administrative offices (10 percent).

Because empirical observations throughout the world indicate that overall economic activity and the consumption of electricity move in lockstep—with an electricity/GDP elasticity of close to one—electric power consumption is considered the single best physical indicator of economic activity. When roughly applied in Vietnam, this indicator suggests the shadow economy averaged about 40 percent of formal GDP from 1997 to 2001 and has been growing over time. Our own estimate is that the share of the shadow economy in GDP increased from 30 percent in 1997 to 51 percent in 2001. According to calculations made for other parts of the world over the period 1989–93 (using electricity as a marker), the unofficial economy weighs in at 44 percent in Africa, 39 percent in Central and South America, and 35 percent in Asia (Friedman and others 2000). Since the scale of unofficial activities in both transition economies and those of the Organization for Economic Cooperation and Development (OECD) appears to grow over time (Schneider and Enste 2000), these figures indicate that the size of the shadow economy in Vietnam is roughly comparable to that in other developing countries.

In a study commissioned by the World Bank on the size of the unofficial economy in 110 OECD and developing countries (Schneider 2002), monetary aggregates used to estimate the size of this economy suggest the sector accounts for about 15 percent of GDP in Vietnam. This estimate seems low, especially in the light of more indepth studies on Vietnam that provide evidence of a significant informal sector. Studies and surveys focusing on the market in land-use rights, for example, indicate that the informal market may well dominate the formal market by a significant margin. To cite two examples, approximately 95 percent of household land in Hanoi is bought and sold outside state law (Institute of Law Research 1999), while the underground market in land-use rights accounts for about 70 percent of the total market (Dinh 2002).

---

income so as to evade taxes; (4) domestic service; (5) smuggling; (6) renting of houses or furniture; (7) secondary and unreported activities of administrative offices, army offices, prisons, reeducation camps, and orphanages; (8) operations of nonprofit institutions, charitable associations, the Red Cross, and the like.

The unofficial stock market in Vietnam is thought to involve more than 1,000 companies with a total market value of about $1 billion—which is six times as much as the official exchange, according to local investment banks (Ha 2003). While the vibrant shadow stock market may help promote the official market by making the new concept of share ownership in Vietnam more socially acceptable, it may also complicate the task of building an orderly stock exchange in the future. The shadow market may nurture an investment culture that is disruptive for the official market. For example, insider information is a prerequisite for investing in the shadow stock market but is prohibited in the official stock exchange.

The D. Phan has measured income underreporting by a specific sector group, particularly public sector employees. Although limited in scope, his study has provided an indirect and thus perhaps a more reliable estimate of the magnitude of the bureaucracy's rent-seeking activity. The D. Phan finds that unreported income by public sector households accounts for no less than half of their reported income, and that household members holding a public sector job are more likely to bring home "unofficial" income (Phan 2001). Several independent calculations all suggest the informal sector in Vietnam constitutes about 50 percent of official GDP.

Intensity of Government Intervention in the Vietnamese Economy

The effective level of government intervention in the economy often bears little relation to the formal level of taxation, ownership, and regulatory activity. Rather, it is a function of both the officially declared or intended level of intervention and of the capacity and the incentives for implementation. Table 2.1 illustrates some of the differences across Asian countries between the *intended* and the *actual* level of intervention in the area of taxation. Interestingly, at the formal level, Vietnam's value-added tax (VAT) is among the lowest in the region, yet the higher efficiency of domestic VAT collections makes the effective rate of taxation one of the highest in the region. By contrast, collection efficiency for the import VAT is poor compared with that in other countries of the region, primarily because of numerous exemptions and problems with customs administration. Effective intervention is also high for the corporate income tax. Whereas the official corporate tax rate is broadly in line with the regional level of taxation, the effective tax rate is much higher

TABLE 2.1
NOTIONAL AND EFFECTIVE LEVEL OF TAXATION
IN SELECTED ASIAN ECONOMIES

	VAT (%)	Domestic VAT		Import VAT		Corporate Income Tax (%)
	Notional level (1)	% of domestic demand (2)	Efficiency (3)[a]	% of imports (4)	Efficiency (5)[b]	(6)
Vietnam	10.0	2.7	0.27	2.2	0.22	32[c]
China	17.0	2.9	0.17	6.8	0.40	33
Indonesia	10.0	1.6	0.16	4.5	0.45	30
Philippines	10.0	1.6	0.16	2.7	0.27	32
Sri Lanka	12.5	1.9	0.15	3.0	0.24	
Bangladesh	15.0	1.2	0.08	8.8	0.59	

a. (2)/(1)
b. (3)/(1)
c. 25% for FIEs.
SOURCES: IMF (2001); Vietnam Business Forum (2002); World Bank Group staff calculations.

because all gains and incomes are taxable, but not all expenses are tax deductible or subject to a cap (Thanh Nguyen 2002).

Certain types of government intervention can have a disproportionately high negative impact on welfare. A case in point is Vietnam's cap on marketing expenses (5 percent of the costs of goods sold)[3] that can be deducted for tax purposes, which is probably unique in the region. This cap discourages companies from aggressively pursuing business opportunities and could be particularly damaging for sectors such as services, where a significant part of the expenses relates to marketing. In addition, local companies are subject to a surcharge of 25 percent on return on equity in excess of 20 percent, which is a major disincentive for companies to grow and become more transparent. Similarly, the system of personal income taxation discourages the training and promotion of Vietnamese to high-paid positions in foreign-invested companies (Thanh Nguyen 2002). In addition, unreasonable restrictions apply to the deductibility of provisions for bad debt. For example, to be deductible for tax purposes, the provision for such debts cannot exceed 20 percent of

---

3. Recently increased to 10 percent.

total outstanding debt, and the debt must be outstanding for at least two years (Vietnam Business Forum 2003: 69–70).

When it comes to regulatory intervention, degree and intensity are more difficult to estimate than is the case for taxation. One problem is that no single measure exists to gauge and monitor the level of regulatory activity and its impact on business. In Vietnam, the problem is compounded by the fact that the country is just beginning to establish a legal framework and a set of rules that can accommodate the market economy. Therefore the level and intensity of legal and regulatory activity are bound to be high. Between 1992 and 1999, for example, legislative efforts included nearly 120 new laws and ordinances, and thousands of implementing regulations and guidelines (Quinn 2002).

More important than the number of laws and regulations is the compliance cost that they impose on business. Although the Enterprise Law, for instance, abolished 150 types of business licenses, shortened the process of establishing an enterprise from 90 days on average to about 15 days, and reduced registration costs from about 10 million Vietnamese dong to about 500,000 Vietnamese dong, more than 150 licenses remain.[4] Furthermore, there has been some reversal in the liberalization of business entry that the Enterprise Law introduced. For example, the government has issued more than 70 legal documents—including 2 laws, 2 ordinances, 13 decrees, and 31 circulars—since 2000. Some of these appear to contradict the letter and the spirit of the Enterprise Law, reintroducing, in disguised form, licenses, capital requirements, and other entry restrictions (CIEM 2002).[5] As a result, costs of market entry have increased to about 45 days and 5.2 million dongs, approximately 84 percent of per capita income (CIEM 2003).

Businesses in Vietnam also have to contend with frequent changes in laws and regulations, often without appreciable results. The Law on Foreign Investment, for instance, was changed four times between 1987 and 2000 but still does not provide an adequate

---

4. On cross-country comparisons in the area of market entry, see Djankov and others (2002).

5. One example is Decree 10/2001/ND-CP on navigation services. Another example is Decree 87/2002/ND-CP, regarding the establishment of consultancy institutions and the supply of consulting services. It states that individuals cannot provide consulting services independently and have to work in a consulting organization.

framework for foreign investment in Vietnam. In addition, the Law on Organization of the National Assembly, the Law on the Organization of the Government, the Law on Organization for People's Councils, the Law on Organization of the People's Courts, and the Law on Organization of the People's Procuracies have been revised by the National Assembly during almost every term.

Rapid change of this nature inevitably spawns inconsistency, contradiction, and ambiguity in the law, which means that new laws will not be in harmony with those already on the books and legal documents will emanate from a multiplicity of sources. The resulting confusion opens the door to bureaucratic discretion, which, in a country in the midst of a major transformation and transition toward a market economy, can be considerable. Discretion is that "gray" area within the confines of rules, regulations, and structural conditions where individual incentives and self-interest are able to gain a foothold.

In Vietnam, discretion also arises from the way new laws are being implemented. New laws typically provide only a framework, leaving it to local governments to work out the details and resolve difficult matters in enforcing legal documents prepared and issued by the ministries at the central level. Sublaws to guide the implementation are usually long in coming, however. Without guiding ministerial circulars, local bodies may be reluctant to move on a decree, even though it has already come into effect. But even if the roles of the various government institutions were clarified and the inconsistencies in the legislation addressed, there would still be substantial room for local authorities to apply their own interpretation to central policies.

In this environment, local officials have different perceptions of how much administrative flexibility they actually have in order to make expenditure decisions and experiment with local development strategies. Some provinces see themselves as agents of the central government, others as representatives of their localities. Some provincial People's Committees simply accept national dictates; others choose the most generous interpretation of a dictate or actively negotiate with higher administrative levels about expenditure decisions and development policies; and still others openly deviate from central norms and devise their own strategies on development issues or social service delivery (Litvack and Rondinelli 1999).

The proliferation of often conflicting rules and regulations in Vietnam reflects in part the conventional wisdom that detailed government laws and regulations can reduce bureaucratic discretion and improve policy implementation. There is, in fact, abundant evidence to the contrary. Very specific and detailed regulations often result in complex laws. If anything, "the possibility of evasion and unintended consequences may sometimes . . . increase as the regulations become more complicated" (Olson 1982).

Government Interventions and Business Informality: Main Survey Findings

Our survey provides a number of measures and observations on the informality of business activities in Vietnam. We use the share of transactions taking place outside the banking system and the share of informal labor contracts as measures of informality at the firm level. These two aspects of informality capture most of what can be regarded as unrecorded transactions whose main purpose typically is to avoid taxes, visibility, and regulatory compliance.

Despite the rapid monetization of the economy, Vietnam continues to operate largely as a cash economy. About 35 percent of broad money is currency outside the banking system (IMF 2002a), which is high by international standards.[6] According to the U.S. Department of Commerce, more than 50 percent of local business transactions are conducted outside the banking system (Vietnam Country Commercial Guide FY2002). Although the 1998 banking law and subsequent campaigns were intended among other things to reduce the country's reliance on cash transactions, so far they have met with limited success.

Figure 2.1 and table 2.2 summarize survey data on cash transactions. Figure 2.1 presents information on bank transactions by ownership and table 2.2 by size. The data suggest that cash is the preferred method of payment within the private sector in Vietnam. Among sample firms, nearly one in every three private enterprises reports that less than 20 percent of its sales and purchases are transacted through the banks. About 45 percent of surveyed private firms have more than 60 percent of their total transactions settled through the banking system. SOEs appear to be somewhat more formal than their private counterparts in this area. Only 22 percent of the surveyed SOEs transact less than 20 percent of their sales, and for 59 percent of this group, settling accounts through banks is the preferred

---

6. In China for example, the ratio was about 13 percent in 2001 (IMF 2002b).

FIGURE 2.1

TRANSACTIONS THROUGH THE BANKING SYSTEM BY TYPE OF OWNERSHIP

Respondents (%)

Transactions (%)

SOURCE: Author calculations based on survey data.

method. The data reveal a tendency for enterprises to cluster at the extreme end of the range, with either very low or relatively high reliance on the banking system. This pattern holds for both state-owned and private companies and indicates the presence of switching costs and externalities related to the use of the banking system.

TABLE 2.2

RELIANCE ON BANK TRANSACTIONS BY FIRM SIZE

(percentage of respondents)

	Number of employees			
Bank transactions (%)	< 25	25–100	101–500	> 500
< 20	35	32	22	16
20–40	5	23	6	0
41–60	19	10	10	16
> 60	41	35	62	68
Total	100	100	100	100
Average (%) of transactions conducted through banks	47	42	58	63

SOURCE: Author calculations based on survey data.

Table 2.2 illustrates that size is important for the degree to which firms rely on the banking system to settle their transactions. The fixed costs of using the banking system for payments are not negligible in Vietnam.[7] They do not, however, seem to be a major determinant of the overall low reliance on the banking system for settling transactions, as the difference between larger and smaller companies in this respect is not very pronounced. Firms with more than 500 employees report conducting about 63 percent of their transactions through the banking system, while firms with fewer than 25 employees put the figure at 47 percent. Sixteen percent of large firms rely almost entirely on cash transactions.

Another aspect of informality explored in the study concerns labor, since labor regulations have considerable bearing on informality in developing countries. Indeed, it has been argued that "of all types of regulations, those related to workers' welfare are the most restrictive and costly in underdeveloped countries (and in many developed countries as well)" (Loyaza 1996: 133). As a result, in many developing countries the additional costs related to labor regulations are the most important component in the overall cost structure (Tokman 1992).

Vietnam has an extensive set of labor regulations. According to indices of labor regulations for 104 developing and developed economies calculated by the World Bank Doing Business project, Vietnam ranks fourteenth in terms of intensity of labor regulations (Botero and others 2002). Given the high intensity of regulations and the limited human resources dedicated to their enforcement, it is not surprising that compliance with labor regulations is poor. According to data from the Vietnam Social Security (VSS), of about 40 million workers only 4 million are covered by social insurance. And of these 4 million, only 380,000 are private sector workers (Belser 2000).[8] A

---

7. For example, one of the largest state-owned banks charges US$2 for payments to enterprises with accounts in a different branch of the bank, and 0.05 percent (minimum $2 and maximum $50) of the transacted amount in the case of payments to accounts in different banks.

8. The Labor Code of Vietnam provides for a certain number of nonwage benefits. Since the adoption of the Labor Code in 1995, contributions to the social insurance fund are mandatory in all enterprises that employ more than 10 workers: employees must pay 5 percent of their wages and employers a further 15 percent of workers' wages. For businesses that employ fewer than 10 people, or for

TABLE 2.3
WORKERS WITH FORMAL LABOR CONTRACTS
AS A PERCENTAGE OF TOTAL LABOR

	Mean	Standard deviation	Mini-mum	Maxi-mum
Ownership				
SOE	97	6	78	100
Private	80	28	0	100
Size (number of employees)				
< 25	81	26	0	100
25–100	85	25	0	100
101–500	89	22	4	100
> 500	92	22	7	100

SOURCE: Author calculations based on survey data.

similar picture emerges from information collected at the firm level. Studies conducted by MPDF (Webster 1999; Webster and Taussig 1999) show that 6 percent of the larger private firms generally sign no contracts at all with their workers, while another 23 percent sign only daily or monthly contracts. Furthermore, in the whole private manufacturing sector, seasonal and part-time workers (for whom no social security contribution needs to be made) represent about 30 percent of the total labor force.

Table 2.3 reports survey data on the average percentage of workers who have formal contracts with their employers, by ownership and firm size. In general, SOEs have higher percentages of workers with formal contracts than do private enterprises. The share of workers with formal contracts increases with firm size. About 4 percent of private firms report having no formal contracts with their workers. For state-owned enterprises in our sample, part-time and seasonal workers represent 34 percent of the total labor force; for private enterprises, part-time and seasonal workers account for 41 percent of the total labor force. All state-owned enterprises in our sample have

---

employees with contracts shorter than three months, social insurance allowances have to be directly included in take-home pay. In addition to social insurance, employers and employees are subject to mandatory health insurance: employers must contribute 2 percent of workers' wages, and employees 1 percent.

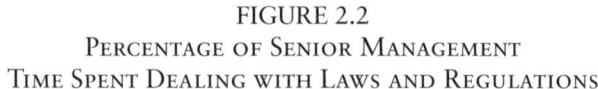

FIGURE 2.2
PERCENTAGE OF SENIOR MANAGEMENT
TIME SPENT DEALING WITH LAWS AND REGULATIONS

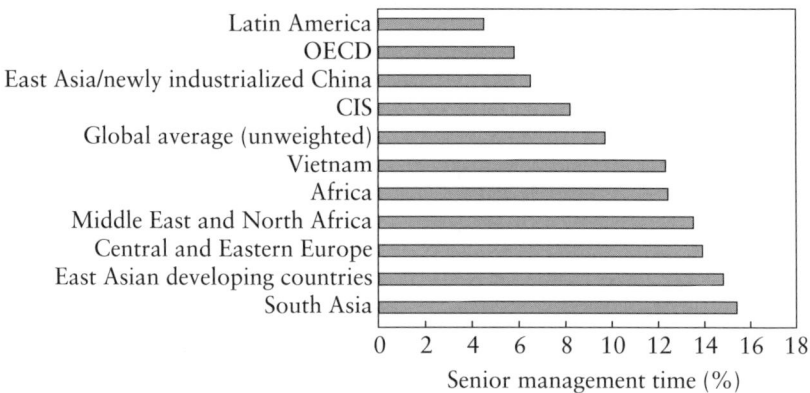

SOURCES: Author calculations based on survey data; Batra, Kaufmann, and Stone (2002).

trade unions, whereas only 43 percent of private enterprises have established trade unions.

We use two indicators to capture the intensity of government regulations: senior management time spent dealing with regulations and government inspections. The number of days that senior management spends per year dealing with requirements imposed by government regulations such as taxes, labor requirements, licensing, and registration (including dealings with officials, completing forms, and so on) is the most comprehensive measure of the intensity of government-business interactions. As such, it also includes the senior management time that enterprises spend in camouflaging noncompliance. Senior management time can thus be endogenous with respect to informality. Enterprises in the sample report spending 28 days per year (about 12 percent) of senior management time, on average, dealing with government regulations.

Figure 2.2 compares time spent on regulatory compliance by Vietnamese firms with results from a World Business Environment Survey. Results from Vietnam seem roughly comparable with results from most developing regions but are significantly higher than for newly industrialized states in East Asia and Latin America. The reported share of management time spent on dealing with regulations

TABLE 2.4
AVERAGE SENIOR MANAGEMENT TIME SPENT DEALING
WITH REGULATIONS, BY OWNERSHIP AND SIZE
(number of days a year)

	Mean	Standard deviation	Minimum	Maximum
Ownership				
SOE	21	18	1	90
Private	30	43	1	360
Size (number of employees)				
< 25	24	19	1	90
25–100	35	63	2	360
101–500	21	20	3	75
> 500	35	45	1	168

SOURCE: Author calculations based on survey data.

in Vietnam is similar to that in China, where, according to a recent World Bank survey, enterprises report spending about 11 percent of managerial time on meeting regulatory requirements. The opportunity cost of time spent on regulatory compliance is less time spent on business issues or (if a firm can afford it) hiring more managers.

We do observe significant differences across ownership and size of firms (table 2.4). Private enterprises tend to spend 9 days more a year on dealing with requirements imposed by regulations than state-owned firms, and the difference is statistically significant at the 5 percent level. There is no clear pattern with respect to size. Surprisingly, however, the largest firms tend to spend relatively more senior management time on dealing with regulations than do smaller firms. With respect to size and ownership, Vietnam shows a different pattern from China, for example. According to a recent World Bank business environment survey in China, small enterprises spend 13.1 percent of their managerial time on regulations compared with 11.3 percent for large firms. China's state enterprises tend to spend a higher percentage of their managerial time on regulations than do domestic private enterprises: 12.2 and 11.5 percent, respectively.

We also observe significant differences in the amount of time senior managers spend on dealing with regulations across localities (figure 2.3). While the main laws and regulations on the business environment are national and apply to all firms irrespective of their

FIGURE 2.3
Average Senior Management Time Spent
Dealing with Regulations, by City or Province
(number of days a year)

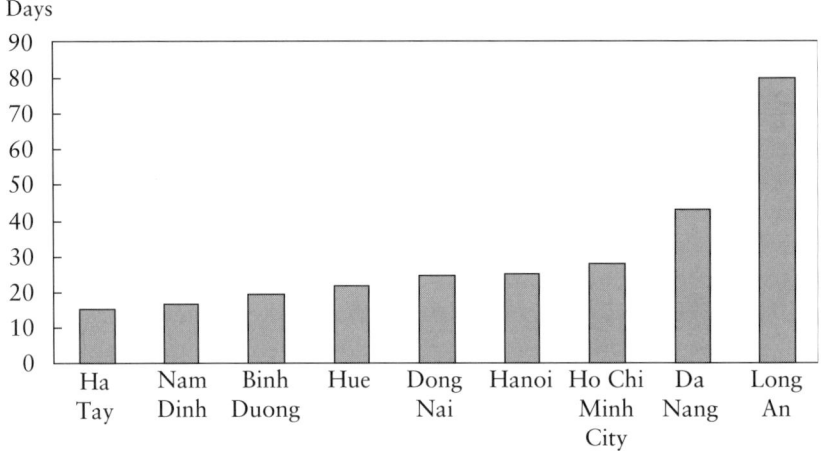

NOTE: Thanh Hoa and Hai Phong were excluded because of too few observations.
SOURCE: Author calculations based on survey data.

location, their implementation varies significantly across provinces, and the system still leaves a lot of discretion to local governments to impose fees, call for additional licenses, and issue local guidelines and subregulations regarding the implementation of national regulations.

The government's enforcement mechanism is proxied by the frequency of government inspections. Surveyed enterprises report receiving 2.3 inspections on average per year. Excluding customs inspections and outliers, private enterprises receive 2.4 inspections a year compared with 2.0 inspections for state-owned enterprises. These estimates are consistent with findings from the VCCI's (2000) report on the implementation of the Enterprise Law, which notes that enterprises were subject to 4 inspections per annum over the three years prior to the survey and that the trend has been declining. If we do not control for outliers, we also find the average number of inspections to be close to four (that is, 3.7). Including customs inspections, the average number of inspections increases to six overall and 6.9 for private enterprises (table 2.5). In contrast to the VCCI report, we find a higher frequency of tax and environment inspections, but a lower frequency of police and labor inspections.

TABLE 2.5
FREQUENCY OF INSPECTIONS PER YEAR BY TYPE AND OWNERSHIP FORM

Ownership	Type of inspection	Mean	Standard deviation	Mini-mum	Maxi-mum
SOE	Tax	0.8	0.9	0	4
	Fire	0.5	0.7	0	3
	Labor	0.4	0.6	0	2
	Sanitation	0.2	0.4	0	2
	Police	0.1	0.3	0	1
	Construction	0.0	0.2	0	1
	Customs	0.03	0.18	0	1
	Other	0.0	0.3	0	2
Total		2.0	2.0	0	7
Private	Tax	1.0	2.1	0	12
	Fire	0.6	0.9	0	5
	Labor	0.3	0.6	0	2
	Sanitation	0.2	0.5	0	3
	Police	0.3	1.2	0	10
	Construction	0.0	0.2	0	2
	Customs	4.5	28.4	0	300
	Other	0.0	0.0	0	0
Total		6.9	29.1	0	302

SOURCE: Author calculations based on survey data.

We also find pronounced differences between inspections of state-owned and private enterprises by police and labor authorities. Private enterprises have the police on their premises more frequently (the difference is statistically significant at the 10 percent level), while state-owned enterprises are subject to more labor inspections (the difference is statistically significant at the 20 percent level). More than half of the sampled enterprises were inspected by the tax authorities in the last year prior to the survey. More than a third (37 percent) were inspected by the fire department and one-quarter by the labor authorities.

The frequency of inspections does not appear to be particularly high in Vietnam when compared with findings from other countries (Morisset and Neso 2002; Coolidge 2003). Nevertheless, private enterprises complained a great deal about the frequency of inspections and the way inspections are conducted. The frequency far exceeds the signals authorities receive about legal violations (VCCI 2000). Enterprises complain that the assessments of the inspection

27

authorities are frequently inaccurate and that inspections can be very disruptive for the operation and reputation of an enterprise (VCCI 2000). Sample enterprises also report that an inspection by the tax authorities typically lasts 4.5 days; inspection by the labor and social authorities, 1.3 days; by the sanitation authorities, 1 day; and by fire and safety, 1 day. It is common for private firms to give government officials cash or gifts when such visits occur.

Exploring the Relationships

In this section, we explore the relationships between informality, government interventions, and relevant firm, industry, and regional characteristics. Although it is difficult to attribute causality to some of these relationships, the findings are potentially useful as they can shed some light on several important questions: What are the main determinants of informality? Do we see systematic differences in the degree of informality with respect to various firm characteristics? Are government interventions such as inspections effective in ensuring better compliance? Do they show a pattern, a certain bias with respect to particular types of companies? Are they associated with rent-seeking?

The two aspects of informality considered here show a positive but weak correlation with each other.[9] Companies that rely more on the banking system tend to have a higher percentage of workers with formal contracts. The positive but weak correlation between these two aspects of informality suggests the importance of both common and individual factors. In both cases we look at factors related to relevant firm characteristics, government interventions, and industry and regional factors.

We use the method of ordered probit to simultaneously explore the effects of the following variables on the propensity of firms to use the banking system to settle their transactions: size, ownership, the share of direct exports in a firm's direct sales, number of government inspections a firm receives a year, the city average of senior management time spent in dealing with regulations, whether a firm's main business is in industry or services, and whether it is located in the North, the South, or the Center of Vietnam (see appendix table 2.9 for technical details).

---

9. Pearson correlation coefficient is 0.14 with a p-value of 0.08.

We find that bigger firms tend to rely more on the banking system, and the coefficient is statistically significant at the 5 percent level. Interestingly, private firms tend to use the banking system to a greater extent than state-owned firms when controlling for the above factors. The coefficient is not statistically significant, however. Enterprises that export directly a higher percentage of their products tend to rely on the banking system to a larger extent, and the coefficient is statistically significant at the conventional 5 percent level. While causality between exports and formality can run in both directions, this finding suggests the importance of openness and interactions with "strangers" in promoting a higher degree of formality.

Frequency of inspections and city averages of senior management time spent dealing with regulations capture the efficacy of the government's enforcement mechanism and the compliance costs that city governments impose on companies in their jurisdictions. We find that frequency of inspections does not have a statistically significant association with the propensity to use banking as opposed to cash transactions. City averages of management time spent dealing with regulations, however, show a statistically significant relationship with the use of bank transactions. Enterprises tend to be less formal (as far as their reliance on the banking system is concerned) in cities where enterprises spend more time dealing with regulations. Industry and regional characteristics do not show a strong relationship with the propensity for bank transactions.

In the case of formal labor contracts, we simultaneously explore the effects of the following variables: size, ownership, the share of casual and seasonal workers in the total labor force, the presence of a trade union or not, the number of government labor inspections a firm receives per year, the city average of senior management time spent in dealing with regulations, and industry and regional characteristics (see appendix table 2.10 for technical details). We find that size is positively associated with formality in the area of labor contracts. The coefficient has very low statistical significance, however. Private firms tend to be more informal: their percentage of formal labor contracts is 11 points lower than the percentage for comparable state-owned firms. The coefficient is statistically significant. Labor inspections have a positive effect on formality in the area of labor. Firms that have been inspected by the labor authorities in the past 12 months have a 6-point higher percentage of workers with formal labor contracts. The association is not significant at the 5 percent level, however. As expected, firms that rely more on seasonal and casual workers have a lower percentage of employees with formal labor contracts, and the association is statistically significant. Firms with trade unions have a 5 point higher percentage of workers with formal labor contracts. The coefficient is not statistically significant, however. Finally, city averages of senior management time spent in dealing with regulations are negatively associated with formality, and the coefficient is significant at the conventional 5 percent level. Firms tend to have a lower percentage of workers with formal contracts in cities where the average compliance costs in terms of management time is higher. Again, industry and regional characteristics do not show any strong pattern in the case of formal labor contracts.

Measurement errors, perhaps omitted variables, and endogeneity can violate some of the standard assumptions of the classical linear regression model and lead to misleading results. For example, research on tax compliance in developing and developed economies has shown that the tax authorities use additional firm-specific information to decide whether to inspect a firm (individual) or not (Andreoni, Erard, and Feinstein 1998). If such information is also linked with formality, the frequency of inspections can be influenced by the level of formality. To test the robustness of our results on formal labor contracts, we estimated the formal contract equation as part of a system of simultaneous equations using the two-stage least-squares method. The other equation has labor inspections as a dependent variable and formal labor contract among the regressors. The simultaneous equations estimates reported in appendix table 2.10 do not differ fundamentally from our earlier results. In terms of statistical significance, the results are similar. All coefficients except the coefficient for size preserve their signs. There are significant differences in the magnitude of some of the coefficients, however. The positive effect of labor inspection on the share of workers with formal contracts is four and a half times greater in the simultaneous equations estimates. We observe significant change in the magnitude of the ownership effects: private firms have on average 14 points lower percentage of formal labor contracts than state-owned firms, which is 3 points less than the earlier estimates. Finally the negative impact of average compliance costs by cities and provinces is almost double our previous estimate.

To summarize our findings on the factors influencing informality, we focus on the factors included both in the equations on banking transactions and on formal labor contracts: size, ownership, inspections, and management time spent on regulations by cities. Our results indicate that size is important in the case of reliance on bank transactions, but not in the case of formal labor contracts when controlling for other factors. Ownership, on the other hand, is not important in the case of bank transactions but has a significant association with firms' propensity to enter into formal contracts with their workers. With respect to the effects of government inspections, we find mixed results. The total number of inspections bears little relationship to a firm's propensity to use banks as opposed to cash transactions. On the other hand, labor inspections tend to have a strong and positive effect on the share of formal contracts, although the statistical significance of this association is not very strong. We found that administrative costs by cities as measured by the average senior management time that enterprises spend on dealing with regulations have a negative and statistically significant impact on both aspects of informality.

The findings suggest that the time senior management spends in dealing with regulatory requirements is important in explaining informality. As mentioned earlier, time spent on compliance with regulatory requirements is the result of the totality of government business interactions. As such it encapsulates the effects of a number of factors. It reflects not only the regulatory burden imposed by government agencies but also the time enterprises spend on camouflaging noncompliance. In this analysis, we tried to isolate the contribution of the government by using cities' averages of the time managers spend on meeting regulatory requirements. We now look at the factors affecting the amount of time managers spend dealing with regulations at the level of individual enterprises. We explore the simultaneous effects of the following variables: size; ownership; growth of the labor force as a proxy for visible financial performance; share of direct exports in total sales; degree of formality as captured by the two variables, share of formal labor contracts in the total labor force and propensity to rely on bank transactions; number of inspections and number of licenses; and industry and regional characteristics (see appendix table 2.11 for technical details).

An important finding is that informality is positively associated with the amount of time senior managers spend dealing with regulations. This runs contrary to the conventional belief that the main raison d'être of informality is to reduce compliance costs. While the conventional belief seems to hold in the case of business entities that are entirely informal, there is no compelling reason for it to hold in the case of semiformal business entities. An appropriate analogy here is compliance with tax regulations. The person who does not file a tax return at all obviously saves the entire compliance cost. By contrast, a person who files a tax return but cheats on it may end up spending considerably more time than a person who files a tax return and does not cheat on it.

Enterprises that can gain most from noncompliance are also likely to spend more management time dealing with regulations. Although it is difficult to find conclusive evidence to this effect, some of our results are consistent with this proposition. For example, the larger enterprises in our sample tend to spend more senior management time dealing with regulations. This is counterintuitive, as large enterprises are expected to have more routinized interactions with the government than smaller enterprises, unless we accept the thesis that larger enterprises have more to gain by spending more time dealing with regulations. We also find that faster-growing and presumably more profitable enterprises tend to spend more senior management time on meeting regulatory requirements. This is not surprising given the punitive taxation of returns in excess of 20 percent. The number of inspections is actually negatively associated with management time spent on dealing with regulations when controlling for the other factors,[10] and the number of licenses an enterprise holds does not have a significant impact on regulatory burden.

On average, private companies tend to spend 10 days more of senior management time in dealing with regulations than do state-owned companies.[11] The difference increases significantly to about 26 days when controlling for size, informality, growth rates, and export orientations. Such a large disparity when controlling for factors, some of which relate to the intensity of direct government interventions and the incentives to evade compliance, suggests that interactions with the government tend to impose a heavier regulatory burden on private enterprises than on state-owned ones.

Is this disparity related to a bias in the way regulations are being enforced? To shed some light on this question, we look for patterns in government inspections with respect to enterprise size, ownership,

---

10. The Pearson correlation between senior management time spent on regulations and number of inspections is positive and significant at the 10 percent level.

11. The correlation coefficient has a *p*-value of 19 percent.

number of licenses, and financial performance. We do not, however, have a good benchmark against which to compare patterns in the way inspections are conducted. Assuming that it is in the public interest that regulations are being complied with, do inspections need to be random to be effective in ensuring maximum compliance? In this case, we should not be able to observe any strong relationships between the frequency of inspections and the various enterprise characteristics. Or do inspections need to be biased against companies that have a statistical propensity to show higher noncompliance in order to achieve their stated public objectives? If this is the case, private and smaller companies, for example, will need to be subject to more frequent labor inspections.

Our analysis of survey data shows that larger companies, faster-growing companies, and companies holding more licenses are inspected more often (see appendix table 2.12 for technical details). What these three characteristics have in common is that they make enterprises more visible, and visibility attracts the attention of authorities, in part in the form of more frequent inspections. Private ownership does not show a statistically strong relationship with frequency of inspections.

In the area of labor law, private companies tend to be inspected less, although they are somewhat less formal in terms of their labor contracts. But overall, we do not find a systematic bias pertaining to ownership in the way inspections are conducted.[12] Tax inspections show a strong and significant positive correlation with a firm's growth rate as measured by growth in the total labor force. Tax inspections also show a positive and statistically significant correlation with the number of licenses a firm holds.

The finding that large and state-owned enterprises are more formal, pay more taxes, and are more frequently inspected could be explained in part by the capacity of government agencies to implement regulations. It is clear from interviews with the authorities that

---

12. It can be argued that it is in the public interest for state-owned enterprises to be subject to a greater public scrutiny than private enterprises. The managers of state-owned enterprises, especially of enterprises that have been given control rights over key economic decisions, face a discrepancy between cash flow and control rights that can result in severe incentive problems. The adequate protection of state ownership rights will thus require more oversight and regulatory control over state-owned enterprises.

local tax administrations (which report directly to the Central Tax Authority rather than to the People's Committees) face severe capacity problems that are adversely affecting the quality of their work. Understaffed and with only a handful of officials capable of following the accounting of complex business transactions, all tax authorities we interviewed claimed that they were forced to be much more selective about the types of auditing practices they engaged in. Similar capacity constraints exist in the area of labor administration. Belser (2000), for example, reports that at the central level, Vietnam Social Security has 15 inspectors to make sure that companies and workers pay their contributions. At the district level, VSS has on average six full-time employees to collect revenues, distribute entitlements, and inspect compliance. With such limited capacity, tax and inspection authorities are likely to focus their attention on the state sector, where larger revenues are at stake, rather than on the smaller and more informal private sector. This may account for the bias toward size when it comes to regulations and inspections. State-owned enterprises in many provinces—but especially Nam Dinh and Long An—have complained vociferously about private sector tax evasion. While certain administrative areas and localities may have a shortage of resources, there is anecdotal evidence that bureaucratic slack is often to blame for excessive interventions and harassment of businesses.[13] The observed anomalies of a shortage of resources in some areas and a slack in others are perpetuated by the practice of distributing government budget not according to needs and amount of work but according to government employees (IFC 2003: 18).

Although administrative capacity needs to be strengthened, it is clearly impossible, undesirable, and impractical for a government to have all the resources it needs to guarantee full compliance with regulatory provisions. Furthermore, those provisions must not be too complex, costly, or unreasonable, or the government will never be in a

---

13. The CEO of a textile factory near Hanoi told us the following story. A decision was made to move the factory from the city center to a new location about 40 kilometers from Hanoi because of easier access to land and incentives by the local governments. Soon after the relocation, the premises became the target of frequent inspections. When the CEO complained to senior government officials, they pleaded for understanding, noting that "there are few enterprises in town but many government officials, and these government officials need to do something." So the higher frequency of government inspections was a simple mathematical problem.

position to enforce full compliance. To promote a culture of compliance, the strengthening of administrative capacity, which does not necessarily imply an increase in the size of the government, needs to go hand in hand with the rationalization of laws and regulations, and greater reliance on incentives, self-regulation, and market mechanisms.

However, rent-seeking may be a dominating motive in the case of government inspections. What kind of pattern in the frequency of inspections would be consistent with rent-seeking? In the rent-seeking scenario, inspectors and noncomplying firms divide the costs associated with noncompliance.[14] Maximization of rents can then be consistent with higher inspections of firms that show a statistical propensity for higher noncompliance, since this will increase the probability of imposing penalties for noncompliance and therefore of creating an opportunity for negotiating a bribe. There is ample anecdotal evidence that negotiation with the tax authority is a common practice in Vietnam. About 8 percent of sample firms reported negotiating with the tax authorities over the applicable rate of taxation. As discussed earlier, however, this pattern is consistent with inspections that are motivated by maximizing compliance, in line with the public interest. Comparing inspections directly with compliance as measured by formality may not necessarily help us discriminate between inspections motivated by rent-seeking and inspections motivated by maximizing compliance, as rent-seeking inspections can also lead to better compliance. Indeed, in specific areas, such as labor regulations, we find that higher frequency of inspections is associated with better compliance. The statistical significance of this relationship, however, is not very strong. A more promising approach may be to explore the relationship between the bribe rate and informality.

When we asked surveyed enterprises to what extent they agreed with the statement that government agencies use regulations as a tool for rent extraction, agreement was stronger among private enterprises.[15] The average bribe rate reported by surveyed companies is 2.8 percent of sales revenues. Private companies in our sample tend

---

14. Rent-seeking does not necessarily imply coercion and extortion by government officials. It is also in the interest of noncomplying firms to bargain on how to split the penalty costs associated with noncompliance with inspecting government officials.

15. The difference between state and private enterprises is significant at the 1 percent level.

TABLE 2.6
REVENUES IN UNOFFICIAL PAYMENTS TO PUBLIC OFFICIALS

Region	Percentage of revenues	Percentage of firms responding
Africa	Not asked	Not asked
MENA	Not asked	Not asked
CEE	5.5	0.9
South Asia	5.0	18.8
East Asia developing countries	4.6	22.7
CIS	3.4	3.4
Latin America	2.0	58.0
East Asia/newly industrialized		
China	0.6	86.3
OECD	0.6	83.0
World average	3.0	38.7
Vietnam	2.8	33.3

SOURCES: Batra, Kaufmann, and Stone (2002); survey data.

to pay higher bribes as a percentage of sales revenues: 3.1 percent as compared with 1.4 percent for SOEs. One-half of the state enterprises and one-third of the private enterprises that provided answers to the questions reported a zero bribe rate. The reported number for the percentage of revenues paid in unofficial payments to public officials in Vietnam is close to the world average of 3 percent, according to the World Business Environment Survey. This is lower than reported rates for Central and Eastern Europe and Southeast Asia, but higher than reported rates for Latin America (see table 2.6). According to a recent World Bank survey on China, Chinese companies report paying about 1.8 percent of their sales "to get things done."

The positive correlation between private ownership and bribe rate could still be consistent with the "law of one price" given that private companies tend to be smaller in terms of their sales revenues. The difference between state-owned and private companies regarding the incidence of corruption is not statistically significant at the 5 percent level, however. The level of bribes is negatively and significantly correlated with size. Figure 2.4 illustrates the regressive nature of the corruption tax. The recent World Bank survey on China reports similar bribe-rate patterns with respect to size and ownership: smaller and private companies tend to pay a larger share of their revenues to officials "to get things done."

FIGURE 2.4
REGRESSIVE NATURE OF THE CORRUPTION TAX

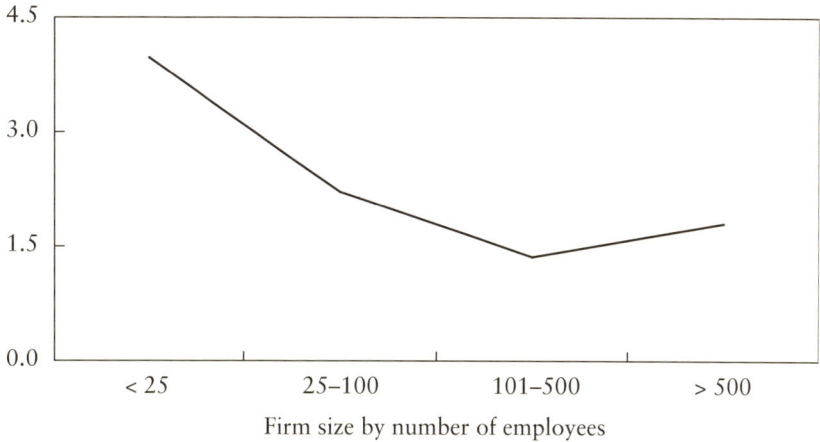

Bribe as a percentage of sales

Firm size by number of employees

A major motivation for going informal is to avoid taxes. Corruption and associated bribery can be viewed as taxes on business activities. An important question is whether informality helps businesses avoid the corruption tax as well. Using regression analysis, we find that a higher degree of formality both in terms of a higher percentage of workers with formal labor contracts and higher reliance on the banking system for settling business transactions is associated with a lower bribe rate, and the result is statistically significant (appendix table 2.13). This points to the benefits of formality in terms of a lower corruption tax. Again it is difficult, and perhaps impossible, to attribute causality in this relationship. Rent-seeking on the part of the bureaucracy can encourage informality, while noncompliance makes companies more vulnerable to extortion and creates a demand for corruption.

Bureaucratic Discretion and Incentives

Bureaucratic discretion is an important factor in determining how regulations are implemented and therefore how burdensome they are to businesses. The current web of rapidly evolving legislation, guiding decrees, and regulations issued by numerous agencies (including

TABLE 2.7
How Is Bureaucratic Discretion Exercised?
(percentage of respondents)

Enterprise response	Central government		Local government	
	Private	SOE	Private	SOE
Interpreted against	23	4	20	11
Decision postponed	64	73	67	82
Interpreted in favor	13	24	13	7
Total	100	100	100	100

SOURCE: Author calculations based on survey data.

central ministries) and local authorities has created not only a confusing tangle of requirements for entrepreneurs but also a large discretionary space for the authorities. To get a feel of how bureaucratic discretion is exercised, we asked enterprises how regulations are interpreted when they contain ambiguities. The results are presented in table 2.7. By and large, government agencies are reluctant to use discretion. The dominant type of bureaucratic behavior in the face of ambiguous regulations is to postpone the decision. The central government seems to be more "entrepreneurial" where state-owned enterprises are concerned: discretion there is more often used to decide in favor of the enterprise if it is state-owned. State-owned enterprises consider local governments more bureaucratic than the central government agencies, whereas private firms see them as slightly less bureaucratic.

The difference between state and private enterprises is statistically significant at the 5 percent level only with respect to the use of discretion by the central authorities. SOEs under central control view the central government as less bureaucratic than the local government, and conversely SOEs under local government control perceive local governments as more entrepreneurial. The better rating of the central government overall is perhaps due to the fact that SOEs under central control dominate our sample. In this context, the views of the private enterprises are less biased and they tend to show less difference from the attitudes of the central and the local government.

Differences in the perceptions of state-owned and private enterprises regarding how discretion is exercised may reflect different official attitudes to state versus private enterprises. Private enterprises in

TABLE 2.8
CEOs' PERCEPTIONS OF GOVERNMENT ATTITUDE
TOWARD PRIVATE BUSINESS
(percent of total)

Current attitude	Negative	Positive	Neutral
Central government	11	52	37
Local government	13	58	29

Trend	Deteriorating	Improving	No major change
Central government	1	87	12
Local government	1	86	13

SOURCE: Author calculations based on survey data.

our sample report that the government's attitude toward private business is largely positive and improving (table 2.8). To further gauge the importance of this factor, we asked managers whether it becomes more difficult to interact with government agencies before important government/party events. Private enterprises show a stronger agreement with the statement that it becomes more difficult to interact with government agencies before important government/party events, and the difference with state-owned enterprises is significant at the 1 percent level. The discrepancy in perceptions suggests that despite the significant improvements in the official attitude toward private business, there still seems to be a residue of a differential approach to state versus private enterprises.

Conclusion

In examining the relationship between government and business and their impact on business informality, we found that private companies tend to be more informal than state-owned enterprises in the areas of reliance on bank transactions and labor relations. Size also has an important association with informality, especially in the case of reliance on bank transactions. The positive and statistically significant association that we find between propensity to export and propensity to use the banking system suggests that openness and dealing with "strangers" are important for promoting a more formal enterprise sector.

Local governments can contribute to higher informality by excessive regulations and cumbersome administrative processes. We find that in cities where enterprises report spending more time dealing with regulatory requirements, they tend to be more informal both with respect to their reliance on banking transactions and propensity to enter into formal labor contracts with their workers. Larger companies, faster-growing companies, and companies holding more licenses (in other words, more visible companies) tend to be inspected more often. Tax inspections in particular show a strong and significant positive correlation with a firm's growth rate as measured by the growth in the total labor force. We do not find an ownership-based bias in the way inspections are conducted.

Our results also show that informality imposes important direct costs on business. More informal companies tend to spend more managerial time dealing with regulations. And higher informality is associated with the payment of more bribes as a percentage of a firm's total revenues. This is an important difference between the intermediate forms of informality examined in this study and firms that are entirely in the informal sector. The latter do not incur direct costs associated with informality but tend to incur significant indirect costs associated with their reduced capacity to obtain public services and participate in markets that rely heavily on information related to formality.

Appendix

TABLE 2.9
ORDERED PROBIT ANALYSIS
OF THE PROPENSITY TO USE THE BANKING SYSTEM

Variable	(1)	(2)
Size (log of number of employees in 2001)	−0.19 (5.35)	−0.20 (5.31)
Ownership dummy (1 is private)	−0.07 (0.08)	−0.22 (0.69)
Share of direct exports in sales	−0.008 (4.32)	−0.007 (3.81)
Number of inspections	0.03 (0.72)	0.027 (0.45)
City average of management time spent dealing with regulations (days per year)	0.01 (3.10)	0.01 (4.16)
Industry controls	No	Yes
City controls	No	Yes
Number of observations	149	149
Log likelihood	−190	−187

NOTE: Probit is modeling the probability of lower reliance on the banking system. Therefore, negative coefficients imply a higher probability of heavier reliance on the banking system to settle transactions. Wald chi-square in parentheses. Dependent variable is the share of transactions going through the banking system.
SOURCE: Author calculations based on survey data. Dependent variable is the share of transactions going through the banking system.

TABLE 2.10

REGRESSION ANALYSIS OF FORMAL LABOR CONTRACTS
AND LABOR INSPECTIONS

Variable	(1)[a]	(2)[b]	(3)[c]	(4)[d]	(5)[e]	(6)[f]
Intercept	95.60	−0.72	93	−0.91	110	−2.03
	(9.95)	(−2.59)	(9.69)	(−3.41)	(5.51)	(−0.86)
Size (log of number of	0.51	0.13	1.22	0.11	−2.41	0.11
of employees in 2001)	(0.27)	(3.9)	(0.63)	(2.63)	(−0.63)	(1.8)
Ownership dummy	−11.50	0.09	−9.8	0.10	−14.2	0.27
(1 is private)	(−2.2)	(0.84)	(−1.82)	(0.83)	(−2.17)	(0.77)
Percentage of casual and	−0.18	0.003	−0.18	0.002	−0.23	0.005
seasonal workers	(−2.35)	(1.55)	(−2.27)	(1.34)	(−2.26)	(0.95)
Number of labor	5.68		5.59		27.4	
inspections	(1.56)		(1.52)		(1.12)	
Percentage of formal		0.002		0.003		0.02
labor contract in		(1.22)		(1.52)		(0.64)
total labor force						
City average of manage-	−0.26	0.008	−0.14	0.01	−0.47	0.01
ment time spent dealing	(−2.01)	(3.01)	(−0.97)	(3.32)	(−1.7)	(1.95)
with regulations						
(days per year)						
Trade union dummy	5.46		4.80		3.39	
(1 if a firm has a	(0.97)		(0.85)		(0.51)	
trade union)						
Industry controls	Yes	Yes	Yes	Yes	No	Yes
City controls	No	No	Yes	Yes	No	No
Number of observations	154	162	154	162	154	154
R-square	0.18	0.24	0.2	0.26	0.15	0.2

NOTE: *t*-statistics in parentheses.
a. Dependent variable is percentage of formal labor contracts in total labor force. Method: OLS.
b. Dependent variable is frequency of labor inspections. Method: OLS.
c. Dependent variable is percentage of formal labor contracts in total labor force. Method: OLS.
d. Dependent variable is frequency of labor inspections. Method: OLS.
e. Dependent variable is percentage of formal labor contracts in total labor force. Method: 2SLS.
f. Dependent variable is frequency of inspections. Method: 2SLS.
SOURCE: Author calculations based on survey data.

TABLE 2.11
REGRESSION ANALYSIS OF SENIOR MANAGEMENT TIME
SPENT DEALING WITH REGULATIONS

Variable	(1)	(2)	(3)
Intercept	54.9	45.1	29.05
	(1.26)	(0.98)	(0.88)
Size (log of number of	17.3	17.6	12.2
employees in 2001)	(2.92)	(2.95)	(2.6)
Ownership dummy (1 is private)	33.06	30.5	25.5
	(1.79)	(1.59)	(1.84)
Employment growth (average	0.81	0.79	0.51
percentage last two years)	(2.64)	(2.48)	(2.36)
Number of inspections	−6.46	−8.11	−1.42
	(−1.81)	(−2.14)	(−0.58)
Percentage of formal labor	−0.84	−0.78	−0.61
contract in total labor force	(−2.59)	(−2.33)	(−2.46)
Propensity for banking	−9.61	−9.59	−3.58
transactions	(−1.84)	(−1.82)	(−0.98)
Number of licenses a firm holds	0.19	0.18	
	(0.09)	(0.07)	
Percentage of direct exports	−0.60	−0.70	−0.45
in total sales	(−2.06)	(−2.25)	(−2.19)
Industry controls	No	Yes	No
City controls	No	Yes	No
Number of observations	50	50	68
R-square	0.34	0.38	0.23

NOTE: t-statistics in parentheses.
SOURCE: Author calculations based on survey data.

TABLE 2.12

REGRESSION ANALYSIS OF FREQUENCY OF GOVERNMENT INSPECTIONS

Variable	(1)	(2)	(3)	(4)	(5)	(6)
Intercept	0.73	1.84	1.83	1.57	0.11	−0.35
	(1.32)	(5.55)	(7.5)	(5.31)	(0.1)	(−0.41)
Size (log of number of	0.27				0.27	0.39
employees in 2001)	(2.23)				(1.49)	(2.79)
Ownership dummy		0.18			0.41	0.79
(1 is private)		(0.46)			(0.64)	(1.68)
Employment growth			0.02		0.02	
(average percentage			(2.12)		(2.03)	
last two years)						
Number of licenses				0.18	0.09	
a firm holds				(2.08)	(1.16)	
Number of observations	168	194	119	137	81	168
R-square	0.03	0.001	0.04	0.03	0.1	0.05

NOTE: t-statistics in parentheses.
SOURCE: Author calculations based on survey data.

TABLE 2.13

CORRUPTION AND INFORMALITY

	Models					
Variable	(1)	(2)	(3)	(4)	(5)	(6)
Intercept	5.76	1.36	6.13	5.29	7.19	9.08
	(3.76)	(1.29)	(3.9)	(4.03)	(2.86)	(2.7)
Size (log of number of	−0.75					−0.46
employees in 2001)	(−2.1)					(−0.98)
Ownership dummy		1.75			1.35	0.91
(1 is private)		(1.49)			(1.02)	(0.58)
Percentage of formal			−0.04		−0.04	−0.03
labor contracts in			(−2.22)		(−1.9)	(−1.55)
total labor force						
Propensity for banking				−0.65	−0.61	−0.61
transactions				(−2.00)	(−1.87)	(−1.52)
Number of observations	78	92	90	80	78	66
R-square	0.05	0.02	0.05	0.05	0.11	0.14

NOTE: Dependent variable is share of payments to officials in sales revenues; t-statistics in parentheses.
SOURCE: Author calculations based on survey data.

3
Markets, Competition, and Evenness of the Playing Field

The degree of informality in Vietnam's enterprise sector varies considerably in relation to ownership, size, and other firm characteristics. High levels of informality can be viewed as a defensive response to excessive regulations, but informality can also have an impact on the evenness of the playing field. As mentioned in chapter 2, if rules and regulations provide for a level playing field, informality gives unfair competitive advantage to noncompliant firms and distorts the allocation of resources. Alternatively, if the playing field is uneven in the critical areas of access to resources and market competition, informality may be a socially efficient response by disadvantaged firms. Thus it is essential to assess informality and the playing field in combination. In chapter 2 we examined systematic differences in informality with respect to size, ownership, and other characteristics of firms in Vietnam. Here we consider the playing field in light of the same characteristics. We highlight key aspects of the business environment such as competition and access to financing, land, and business services.

Markets and Competition

Since a primary concern of entrepreneurs is market entry and competition, we explore the structure of market relationships of Vietnam's private and state-owned firms and the factors responsible for competitive strength in the market. Our survey results on the structure of input and output markets for private and state-owned firms (table 3.1) show no significant difference in the extent of their domestic market. Both types of enterprises have about an equal reach in city, provincial, and national markets, although SOEs have a somewhat stronger presence nationally. Of the output of private firms in

TABLE 3.1
STRUCTURE OF INPUT AND OUTPUT
(percent)

How handled	Output		Input	
	Private	SOEs	Private	SOEs
Sold/purchased domestically	78	84	71	75
Within city	23	30	21	26
Within province	23	18	22	13
Within nation	31	37	28	36
Exported/imported	22	16	29	25
Directly	14	15	18	18
Indirectly	8	1	11	7

SOURCE: Author calculations based on survey data.

our sample, 78 percent is sold domestically, 14 percent is exported directly, and 8 percent is exported indirectly. Sample SOEs show a higher orientation to the local market, with about 84 percent of the output being sold domestically. External trade accounts for a larger share of private firms' total input and output. In particular, private enterprises have a larger share of indirect trade, both on the export and on the import side. The level of informality in terms of reliance on the banking system for conducting business transactions and share of workers with formal labor contracts shows any particular relationship with share of exports or imports only. More formal companies tend to have higher shares of exports or imports in their outputs or inputs.

Although private companies export a greater proportion of their output than do SOEs, a smaller percentage of private firms engage directly in trading (table 3.2). This suggests a higher degree of specialization in external markets among these companies. In domestic output markets, about half of the private firms serve the needs of Vietnamese individuals, compared with 27 percent of SOEs. The SOEs' main customers and suppliers are other SOEs, which is to be expected given the state sector's dominant share in industry and most of the services. Likewise, private enterprises tend to rely on other private enterprises more than SOEs for their customers and suppliers. This means the domestic enterprise sector continues to be segmented. The mutual dependence between state and private enterprises is significant, however, and exceeds their respective dependence on other

TABLE 3.2
MAIN CUSTOMERS AND SUPPLIERS
(percentage of respondents)

Customer/supplier	Output		Input	
	Private	SOEs	Private	SOEs
Foreign				
Direct	20	32	29	47
Indirectly	12	6	25	27
Domestic enterprises				
SOEs	37	62	41	74
Private	39	29	58	58
Foreign-invested	23	29	20	8
Governments			3	3
Central	5	21		
Local	14	15		
Households	49	27	14	3

SOURCE: Author calculations based on survey data.

sectors, including foreign companies. A higher share of SOEs in our sample cited the central government as their main customer, but interestingly, about the same percentage of private and state firms have local governments as important customers. Thus it appears that domestic private firms are relatively well integrated in the economy.[1]

Compared with private firms surveyed in China, however, those in Vietnam seem to be less integrated in the domestic economy. When asked about buyers, for example, 26 percent of the Chinese private firms indicated they sell mainly to government agencies, 46 percent to SOEs, and 42 percent to foreign companies. As for their main suppliers, 45 percent of Chinese private firms were supplied by SOEs, 58 percent by private firms, and 39 percent by foreign firms.

Table 3.3 provides a summary of the main competitors of private firms and SOEs in our sample. Private firms and SOEs alike appear to operate in highly competitive markets, as only 10 percent indicated that they have no competitors. Most of the private firms perceive

---

1. For historical and policy reasons, the private sector has almost no representatives in heavy industry, infrastructure, and telecom. Therefore, there is significant segmentation at the subsectoral level.

TABLE 3.3
MAIN COMPETITORS OF SAMPLE FIRMS
(percentage of firms in the sample)

Competitors	Private	SOEs
None	10	10
Domestic SME private firms	55	44
Domestic large private firms	23	8
SOEs	29	50
Foreign companies	16	18
Smuggled goods	13	27

SOURCE: Author calculations based on survey data.

other private firms as main competitors. Similarly, 50 percent of the SOEs see other SOEs as their main competitors. The data suggest a significant degree of competition between private firms and SOEs, with more state firms perceiving private enterprises as their main competitors than vice versa. At the same time, there is significant regional variation. In the North, 31 percent of the private firms consider SOEs their main competitors; in the Central part of the country, the figure is 38 percent; and in the South only 5 percent of private companies perceive SOEs as main competitors.

In comparison with China, Vietnam appears to have more direct competition between private firms and SOEs. In a survey of domestic private firms in China (Gregory, Tenev, and Wagle 2000), only 12 percent of the CEOs interviewed thought state firms were their competitors. The degree of competition between SOEs and private companies in Vietnam is similar to that in some Eastern European transition economies. This higher competition may be due to the underindustrialization of the Vietnamese economy, in which SOEs themselves are relatively small.

Interestingly, the level of competition between the sample private firms and large private firms is much lower, which suggests some degree of product differentiation between large private firms and SMEs. The weak competition between large private firms and SOEs and private SMEs is perhaps due to the fact that few private firms have become large companies. It may also explain why these private companies became large in the first place. According to our survey results, smuggled goods are hurting SOEs more than private enterprises.

TABLE 3.4
ADVANTAGES OF MAIN COMPETITORS
(percentage of respondents)

Advantages	Private	SOEs
Low price	60	64
Advanced technology	26	39
Government supports	21	13
Better quality	20	30

SOURCE: Author calculations based on survey data.

To summarize, the Vietnamese domestic private sector seems to be reasonably integrated into the economy, as revealed by its trading and competition relationships. The relatively high degree of direct competition between private and state firms can perhaps be explained by the low level of industrialization in Vietnam. This is supported by the finding that direct competition with the foreign sector is low. Foreign investment, particularly in the past, used to be primarily in capital-intensive import-substitution industries, in partnership with larger state companies. In comparison with China, Vietnam seems to have a less integrated private sector in terms of trading relationships with the rest of the economy and a private sector that seems to compete more directly with the state sector.

Table 3.4 presents sample firms' perceptions of the main strengths of their competitors. Both SOEs and private firms tend to view price as the main tool for gaining competitive advantage. More SOEs than private firms view advanced technology as the source of their respective competitors' strength. By contrast, more private firms than SOEs regard government support as the source of their competitors' advantage. The pattern is similar for data presented by business forms and by labor size.

The next question we investigated was whether a relationship exists between the type of main competitor and the source of competitive strength. Private enterprises that cite domestic private SMEs as their main competitors also cite low price as the main source of competitive strength (table 3.5). Similarly, foreign-invested enterprises as competitors correlate with advanced technology as the competitive advantage, while large domestic private enterprises correlate with advanced technology and government support. The largest correlation coefficient is between SOEs as main competitors and government

INFORMALITY AND THE PLAYING FIELD

TABLE 3.5
CORRELATIONS BETWEEN TYPE OF COMPETITOR AND COMPETITOR'S
STRENGTH AMONG PRIVATE ENTERPRISES IN THE SAMPLE

Competitor	Low price	Tech-nology	Government support	Quality
Private SMEs	0.188	0.005	−0.039	0.026
	< .0001	0.8947	0.3297	0.5182
FIEs	−0.073	0.208	0.041	0.000
	0.0689	< .0001	0.3035	0.9918
Large private enterprises	0.074	0.099	0.101	−0.051
	0.0649	0.0137	0.0119	0.202
SOEs	−0.112	0.121	0.373	−0.018
	0.0052	0.0025	< .0001	0.6544
Smuggling	0.189	−0.067	−0.013	−0.062
	< .0001	0.0969	0.7433	0.121

NOTE: *p*-values below correlation coefficients.
SOURCE: Author calculations based on survey data.

support as a source of competitive strength. SOEs as main competitors also correlate positively with advanced technology and negatively with low price as competitive advantages. Large private enterprises as main competitors of private firms correlate positively and significantly with government support as a source of competitive advantage. For SOEs, the only statistically significant correlation is between foreign-invested enterprises as main competitors and advanced technology as the main competitive strength.

In the view of both private and state firms, unfair competition is one of the largest impediments in the business environment. To determine what factors contribute to this perception, we looked at the type of competitors and at the sources of competitors' strength. For private enterprises, the perception of unfair competition is positively and significantly correlated with (in declining order of magnitude of the correlation coefficient) smuggled goods (on average, competition with smuggled goods increases the index of perception of unfair competition by 0.72—with a mean value of 2.59 on a scale from 1 to 4), competition with large private companies (which increases the index by 0.44), competition with SOEs (which increases the index by 0.25), and among competitive strengths, with government support (which increases the index by 0.30).

Concern about unfair competition is equally strong among SOEs, but it seems to be related to different factors. Among types of competitors, perception of unfair competition is positively and significantly correlated with foreign-invested enterprises. Private SMEs as the main SOE competitors are also highly correlated with perceptions about unfair competition, but the coefficient is not statistically significant. Looking at the areas of competitive strength, low prices and advanced technology are positively and significantly correlated with perceptions about unfair competition. Thus the perception about unfair competition is widespread in Vietnam and reflects perhaps the different regimes of operations for private, state-owned, and foreign-invested companies.

Demand for Business Services and the Importance of Social and Business Networks

Gaining competitive strengths is typically associated with building capacities in the areas of marketing, information processing, management technologies, and knowledge about the regulatory environment and prospective suppliers and customers. The market for business services develops in response to such needs. We asked sample enterprises about their effective demand for legal, information technology (IT), accounting, marketing, and other services and the main channels for obtaining those services.

As figure 3.1 shows, the level of consumption of business services is strikingly different for private firms and SOEs in our sample. We found that private enterprises buy far fewer services than the SOEs. One-fifth of sampled private enterprises bought information services, while one-sixth bought finance-accounting services. The shares of private enterprises that used training services, IT-MIS services, technical assistance, and consultancy services were roughly the same, about 11 percent each. Very few respondents said that they had bought advisory and marketing services. At the same time, about 40 percent of surveyed SOEs have purchased information and training services, and about a third have obtained IT-MIS, technical, and consultancy services from outsiders. Legal services were the least bought, purchased by only one-sixth of the SOE respondents and 8 percent of private enterprises.

However, social networks as providers of business services seem to be more important for private enterprises than for state-owned

FIGURE 3.1
PURCHASE OF BUSINESS SERVICES, BY OWNERSHIP

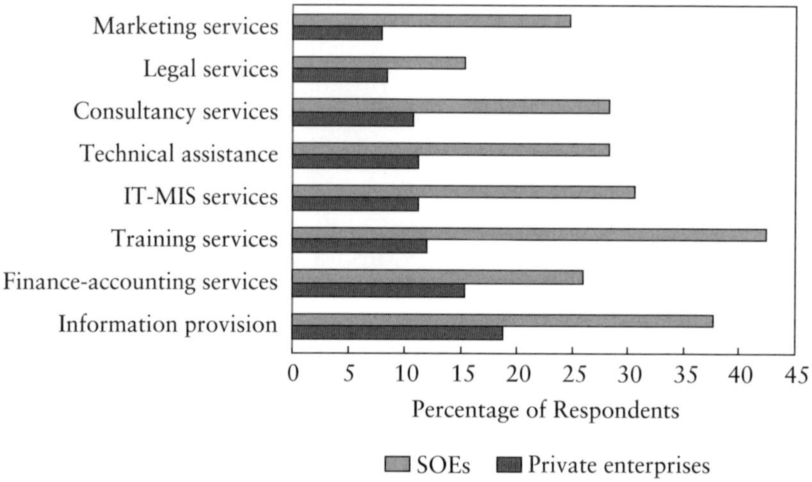

SOURCE: Author calculations based on survey data.

ones. Nearly three-quarters of sampled private enterprises used in-house services or obtained business services from friends, family, or other special unofficial connections. Both private and state enterprises cited some need for assistance in this area. In fact, private enterprises demonstrated a greater need for such "in-kind" services than did the state enterprises. More than half of the private enterprises went to friends and other personal connections to get information (56 percent), and over one-third got help with finance and accounting (36 percent). The corresponding figures for the state enterprises are about one-fifth (21 percent) and one-sixth (17 percent), respectively. About 19 percent of private firms responded that they consult friends and family on laws and regulations compared with 8 percent of state-owned firms (difference in means statistically significant at the 0.01 level). Private enterprises rely more on "informal" and in-kind business services than SOEs in every service category except for training and IT (figure 3.2).

Since, in general, social networks play a more important role for private versus state enterprises, we asked firms to rank the importance of personal (family and friends) relations in the following business activities: bargaining with officials, source of capital, firms'

FIGURE 3.2
INFORMALITY ACROSS SERVICES AND OWNERSHIP

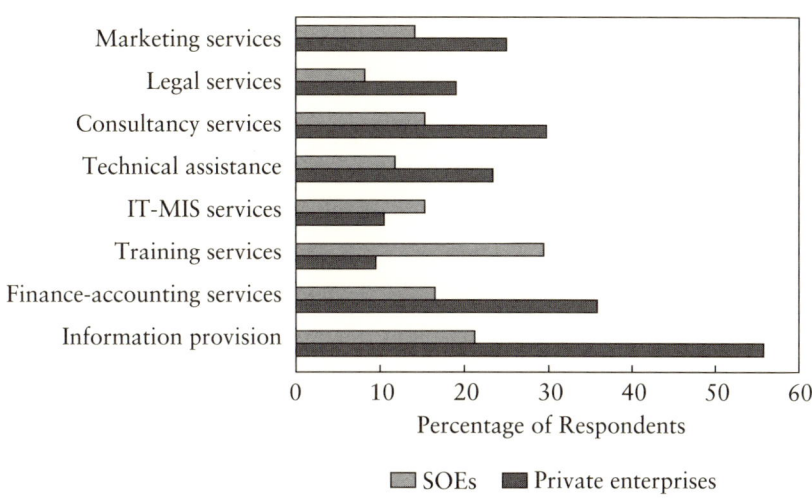

SOURCE: Author calculations based on survey data.

internal problems, bargaining with banks, sales, and business services (table 3.6). In each category, private enterprises ranked the importance of friends and family higher than did state-owned enterprises.[2]

Business services are often provided by nongovernment public organizations such as business associations. These services provide selective incentives for members and thus play an important role in collective action. As our interviews confirmed, private entrepreneurs are reluctant to join business associations. One-fourth of the private enterprises and half of SOEs in our survey were members of at least one business association/organization.[3]

Interviews with private enterprises reveal some of the reasons for this reluctance to join business associations. The two government-run private sector support organizations mentioned in particular were the Vietnam Cooperative Alliance and VCCI. One of their functions is to serve as a link between the government and private enterprises and to provide support services to the sector. Respondents

---

2. See also McMillan and Woodruff 1998.

3. The difference is statistically significant at the 0.01 level.

TABLE 3.6
PERCENTAGE OF FIRMS VIEWING PERSONAL
RELATIONS AS VERY IMPORTANT

Area	Private	SOEs
Bargaining with officials	23	18
Source of capital	49	22
Firm's internal problems	32	19
Bargaining with banks	32	20
Sales	38	22
Business services	26	20

SOURCE: Author calculations based on survey data.

found the performance of the Vietnam Cooperative Alliance to be weak. Although VCCI plays an active role in organizing seminars and some training programs, many private enterprises do not use such programs, nor are they aware of VCCI's training services, which is particularly the case in the poorer provinces. Contacts with some members, especially the ones located outside Hanoi, are sporadic. Some enterprises receive nothing from VCCI except two issues of a newspaper every month despite having paid membership fees, and some find the costs of VCCI courses too high.

It seems that SOEs derive more benefits from membership in associations. A primary benefit that CEOs of both private and state enterprises expect is information. Among the CEOs of private enterprises, 20 percent said that associations/organizations supplied information about technology; 13 percent obtained the names and addresses of clients, suppliers, and competitors; 8 percent gained access to capital sources; and 10 percent were able to establish the creditworthiness of buyers and suppliers. The corresponding figures from the state sector were consistently higher: a third of SOEs mentioned technology, 26 percent the names and addresses of partners and competitors, and 16 percent the creditworthiness of buyers and suppliers (see figure 3.3).

Not only are state enterprises more likely to be members of business associations, but they also belong to stronger informal business networks. Table 3.7 presents data on the strength of business networks in three areas: spreading information about business disputes, discovery of cheating, and ostracism. SOEs consistently express higher effectiveness for their networks.

FIGURE 3.3
MAIN BENEFITS OF MEMBERSHIP IN BUSINESS ASSOCIATIONS

SOURCE: Author calculations based on survey data.

Private enterprises resort less often to the market for the provision of business services. They tend to rely more on social networks to obtain legal advice, information, marketing, and other services. State-owned enterprises on the other hand, are more likely to be members of business associations and obtain business services as a

TABLE 3.7
STRENGTH OF BUSINESS NETWORKS BY FORM OF OWNERSHIP

Strength	Private	SOEs
Spreading of information about business disputes	2.55	2.91
Discovery of cheating	2.62	2.80
Ostracism by business networks	2.43	2.57
Overall network strength	2.51	2.75

NOTE: Questions were asked about the strength of business networks in the three areas cited. Numerical values were assigned as follows: 4, strongly agree; 3, agree; 2, disagree; and 1, strongly disagree. Results shown are statistically significant at 0.01 level.
SOURCE: Author calculations based on survey data.

TABLE 3.8
LOW USE OF THE LEGAL SYSTEM

	Private firms	SOEs
With business disputes	17	13
Percentage brought cases to court	29	23
Number of respondents	141	57

SOURCE: Author calculations based on survey data.

result of such membership. State-owned enterprises also belong to stronger informal business networks. Since the effectiveness of social networks tends to depend on geographical proximity and close and regular contacts, the greater reliance of state-owned enterprises on formal markets and on formal and informal business networks is likely to give state enterprises a competitive advantage in market transactions over longer distances.

This advantage is reinforced by evidence suggesting that the legal system in Vietnam tends to be more reliable when both the plaintiff and the defendant are from the same city/village. Out of 30 firms in our sample that have had business disputes, only 8 decided to bring cases to the courts (table 3.8). SOEs have a higher propensity to enter into business disputes but a lower propensity to bring those disputes to the court system. Most of the firms (about 60 percent) report using no outside agency to assist in resolving business disputes. About 10 percent of the firms have used arbitrators/mediators, and 9 percent have used the local government to assist in the resolution of business disputes.

Controlling for size, ownership, percentage of receivables in arrears, business network strength, and social network strength, we find that that the higher the percentage of customers located within city, the higher the enterprise's propensity to bring disputes to court (see appendix table 3.13 for technical details).[4] This suggests that the

---

4. We also find that private ownership is negatively but insignificantly associated with court disputes. Size is important: larger companies are more likely to bring cases to court. This may be related to high fixed costs of using the legal system, which larger companies can afford, and the higher stakes involved in the case of larger companies. Network strength is negatively associated with propensity to bring disputes to court, suggesting that business networks may act as substitutes for the court system. The result is not statistically significant, however. The

legal system is more reliable closer to home, a conjecture supported by responses to the question about whether managers agree with the statement "Disputes with customer/supplier from my city/village are easier to resolve." About 56 percent of respondents agreed with the statement, and 42 percent had no opinion. No firm that had business disputes or had brought business disputes to court disagreed with the statement.

This feature of the Vietnamese legal system greatly reduces its relevance for private enterprises. It is precisely at long distance and correspondingly in the case of more anonymous transactions that the effectiveness of the court system is of great importance. At shorter distances, private enterprises can rely to a greater extent on the strength of their social networks to regulate the parameters of their market exchanges. The larger percentage of nationwide customers and suppliers for state-owned enterprises in comparison with private ones may be related to these differences.

As Quinn (2002) among others has pointed out, Vietnam is currently facing several difficulties in developing a national court system. The main tension is between the national jurisdiction of the People's Court judgments and the fact that the enforcement of decisions falls under the rubric of local governments. This reduces the ability of People's Courts to develop a strong national court system. The decision to actually enforce a judgment is left to the local government in the jurisdiction where the company finds itself. The authority of the Ministry of Justice seems to be particularly limited where the local party is a favored state enterprise (Quinn 2002). As a result, the ratio of judgments that are not enforced in Vietnam is high, estimated at 37 percent of all judgments.

Access to Capital

Businesses need access to reliable sources of financing in order to be able to take advantage of market opportunities, expand, and compete successfully in the marketplace. Table 3.9 presents data on sources of financing for sample firms. Retained earnings appear to be the major

---

percentage of receivables in arrears is also not statistically significant. We find that the level of informality in terms of reliance on the banking system or percentage of workers with formal contracts does not show a strong association with a firm's propensity to bring cases to the courts.

TABLE 3.9
STRUCTURE OF FINANCING
(percentage of total financing)

Source	Vietnam (private)		Comparators					Vietnam (SOEs)	
	At start	At survey date	China	East Asia[a]	CIS	CEE	OECD	At start	At survey date
Equity	77.1	69.2	56.6	33.9	53.9	70.5	39.1	48.0	38.0
Personal savings/self-generated funds	61.4	57.3							
Savings from friends and family	8.6	7.2	3.0	5.0	4.5	4.0	1.3		
Institutional investors	7.1	4.7	7.5	3.9	10.3	2.7	10.8		
Debt	22.6	30.2							
Friends and family	6.6	5.7	2.9	4.9	4.1	3.3	1.0		
Informal moneylender	2.6	2.9	6.3	1.7	2.5	1.6	2.3		
Banks	11.0	15.4	9.4	20.5	13.5	5.2	16.6	28.0	36.0
Government loan program	0.1	0.3	1.1	0.4	4.6	7.4	2.0		1.1
Borrowed from suppliers	1.8	3.8	2.8	3.2	4.6	5.8	4.8	1.1	1.7
Borrowed from clients	0.8	2.1						1.3	1.8
Other	0.3	0.6						21.6	22.0
Total	100	100						100	100

a. Developing countries.
SOURCES: Survey data; Batra, Kaufmann, and Stone (2002).

source of financing for private firms in Vietnam at present, accounting for 70 percent of total financing. Commercial banks, the second largest source, provide 11 percent of total financing at establishment and 15.4 percent at survey date. Moneylenders finance less than 3 percent of the start-up costs and current assets of the surveyed firms. The informal credit provided by friends, family, and informal lenders accounts for about 9 percent of total firm assets, which appears to be consistent with a recent GSO estimate.[5] As can be seen from table 3.9, there are no significant changes in the financial structure between the present period and time of establishment. As to be expected, the average debt-to-equity ratio increases somewhat with debt from commercial banks and trading partners substituting for retained earning and personal savings. SOEs are more leveraged and rely on fewer financing sources than private enterprises.

As country comparisons suggest, there is nothing unique about the financial structure of Vietnamese private firms or about how it relates to the level of development of the private sector or of the financial system. Across countries, the level of development seems to have little impact: SMEs in countries at very different levels of development can have a similar financial structure, while those in countries at a similar level of development can show quite different financing patterns in their private sectors.

When asked about their nonbank sources of financing, 32 percent of the respondents in our sample reported that lack of access to outside equity is a major constraint, while a further 41 percent called it a moderate constraint (figure 3.4). The firms also reported having difficulty in attracting strategic partners and investors, with 35 percent viewing this as a major constraint to their growth. About 11 percent of the survey firms that are growing have formed joint ventures with other companies or with their clients. Joint ventures between private enterprises and foreign partners are very rare at present, however, accounting for only 8 percent of projects and merely 2 percent of the FDI capital commitments (CIEM 2000: 42). While there seems to be a strong demand for nonbank equity and strategic partnering, the demand for access to equipment finance leasing and specialized export finance is somewhat lower. Only about 15 percent of sample firms see the lack of access to these sources as a major constraint, but these are likely to be among the more dynamic and sophisticated private firms.

---

5. According to a GSO study, in 2000 the informal credit market supplied 8–9 percent of development capital for the country as a whole (www.vneconomy.vn).

FIGURE 3.4
NONBANK SOURCES OF FINANCING

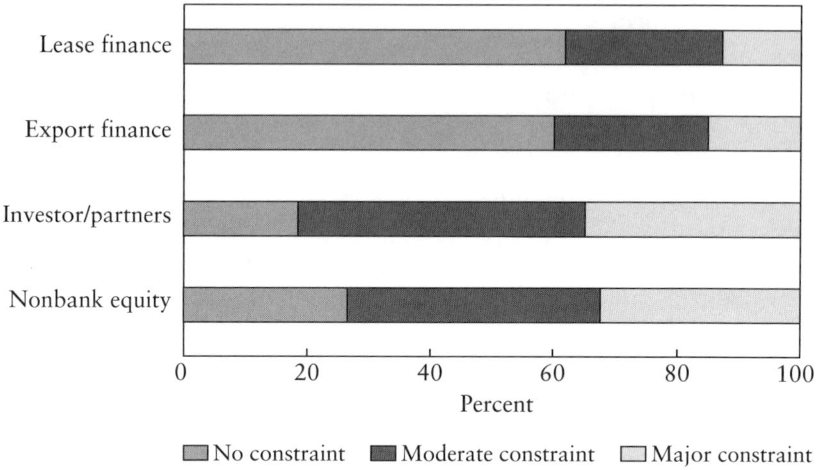

Percent

☐ No constraint ■ Moderate constraint ☐ Major constraint

SOURCE: Author calculations based on survey data.

Enterprises make capital contribution mainly in cash. Capital mobilization in the form of assets is limited. This is largely due to the weak regime of property rights related to land and intangible assets. Weak enforcement and protection of intellectual property rights and complicated and costly registration procedures concerning industrial property rights have made the capital contribution in the form of intangible assets difficult to implement or unattractive (IFC 2003: 8). As the next section discusses in greater detail, the lack of a certificate of land-use rights and the unclear and costly procedure for transferring land-use rights from one user to another and between residential and commercial land use have made the capital contribution in the form of land-use rights difficult to implement.

A comparison of the sources of loan financing for private and state enterprises (figure 3.5) confirms that the financial market in Vietnam is still segmented. Whereas about two-thirds of private enterprises have borrowed money in the past five years, the corresponding number for SOEs is close to 90 percent. Private enterprises report that state-owned commercial banks (SOCBs) and family and friends are about equally important as sources of financing, with about 42 percent of the private firms having relied on these two sources in the past

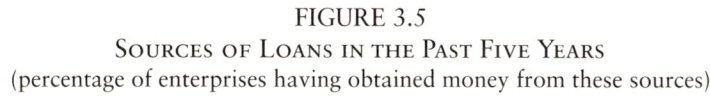

FIGURE 3.5
SOURCES OF LOANS IN THE PAST FIVE YEARS
(percentage of enterprises having obtained money from these sources)

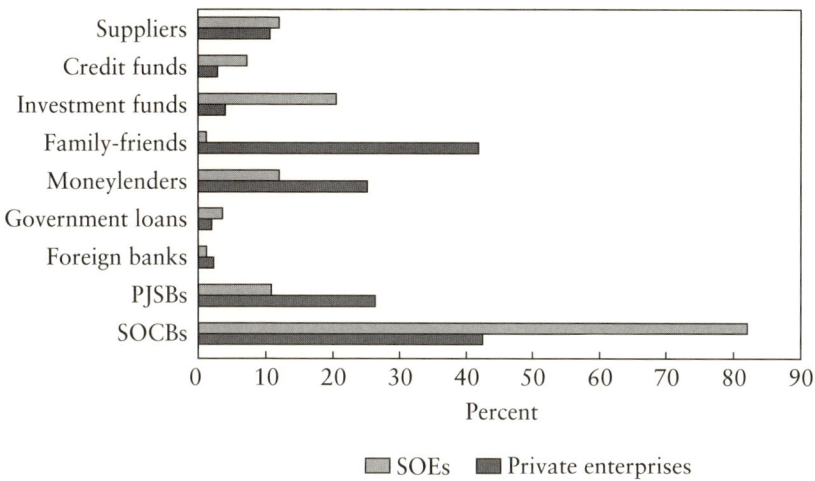

SOURCE: Author calculations based on survey data.

five years. Private joint-stock banks (PJSBs) and moneylenders are next in importance, with 26 and 25 percent of private firms, respectively.

SOE financing preferences are quite different. Almost any SOE that has borrowed over the past five years has relied on a state-owned bank. Second on the list for SOEs are investment funds, which 20 percent cite as a source of financing in the past five years. Moneylenders are the third most important source of financing, with 12 percent having borrowed from them in the past five years. Obviously, the informal credit market is an important source of financing for private firms and SOEs despite its small share in total financing. Because of the high costs associated with informal lending, enterprises typically tend to resort to this source on a short-term basis and for small loans. Private enterprises tend to avoid relying on the informal loan market because of the high cost. Yet they value other aspects of raising capital this way, such as its speed and lack of collateral requirements, service fees, or strict borrowing procedures.

In sum, firms face a segmented financial market with differential access to and preferences for various sources of loan financing among

61

SOEs and private firms. SOEs tend to prefer (have better access to) state-owned commercial banks, investment funds, and government loan programs, while private firms rely more on joint stock banks, family and friends, and moneylenders.

To explain the differences in access to bank loans, we used regression analysis to explore the importance of size (logarithm of number of employees), profitability (profit margins), and possession of titles over land-use rights (certificates of land-use rights, or CLURs). Results appear in appendix table 3.14.

For state-owned enterprises, none of the control factors seems to be an important determinant of bank borrowing. Profitability is even negatively associated with the share of bank loans in total financing but is statistically insignificant. For private enterprises, bigger size, higher profit margins, and possession of CLURs "increase" bank borrowing. Size and profitability are also significant at the 1 percent level. The pooled regression shows that private ownership is associated with a decrease in the share of bank loans in total financing by 11 percent when controlling for size, by 18 percent when controlling for profitability, by 16 percent when controlling for possession of CLURs, and by 14 percent when controlling for all of these factors.

These findings suggest that private enterprises face a very different environment from state-owned enterprises when it comes to accessing bank financing. Factors such as size and profitability that are normally associated with lending practices based on commercial criteria are important in the case of private enterprises but insignificant in the case of state-owned enterprises. Perhaps the implicit or explicit guarantees associated with state ownership sever the links between performance and firm size, on one hand, and access to bank financing, on the other. We do not find the level of informality as reflected in firms' reliance on the banking system for executing business transactions and the share of formal labor contracts in the total labor force to be significantly associated with a firm's propensity to use bank loans.

There does appear to be a significant difference between the way SOCBs and PJSBs approach lending to private firms. SOCBs report that 59 percent of their private borrowers have a CLUR, while the corresponding figure for PJSBs is only 40 percent (figure 3.6).[6] In terms of collateral, PJSBs appears to take a higher risk, but it should

---

6. Similarly, a JBIC study has found that 58.4 percent of private firms with access to finance possess land-use rights (JBIC 2002:52).

FIGURE 3.6
BORROWING AND CLUR

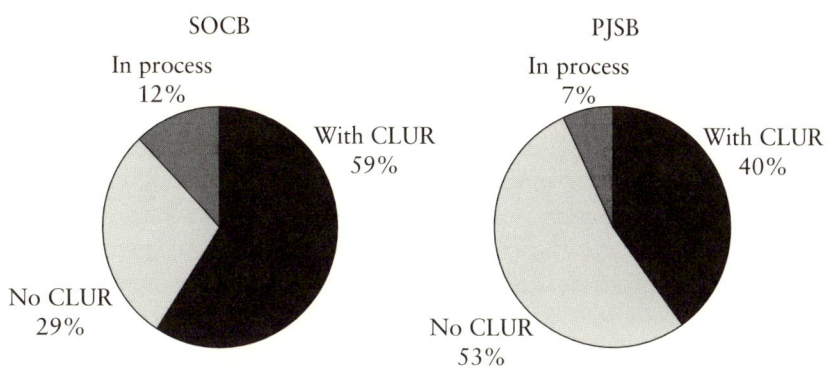

SOURCE: Author calculations based on survey data.

be borne in mind that 70 percent of the firms without a CLUR have made profits in the past two years.

Survey results also reveal that SOCBs are more conservative than PJSBs when it comes to using profitability as a criterion for lending (figure 3.7). Whereas 72 percent of firms that have borrowed from

FIGURE 3.7
BORROWING AND PROFITABILITY

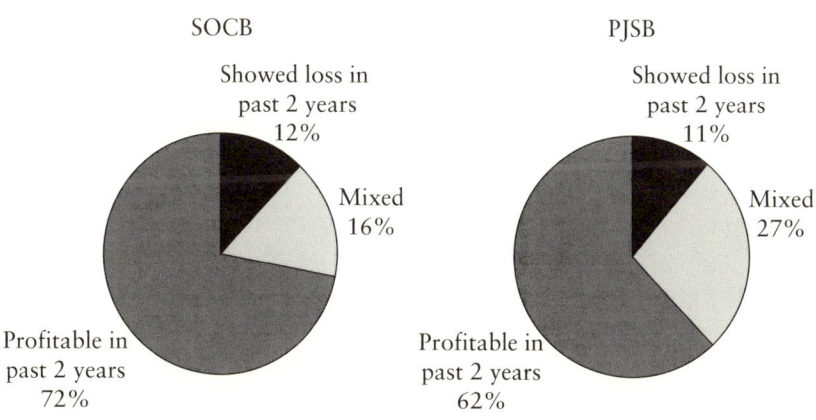

SOURCE: Author calculations based on survey data.

TABLE 3.10
ACCESS TO BANK CREDIT BY FIRM SIZE
(percentage of respondents)

	Private enterprises		State-owned enterprises	
Number of employees	SOCB	PJSB	SOCB	PJSB
< 50	36.2	19.1	66.7	17.0
50–99	57.1	34.3	90.0	10.0
100–199	52.6	29.8	78.6	8.0
> 200	42.4	26.2	81.9	9.0

SOURCE: Author calculations based on survey data.

SOCBs have been profitable in the past two years, only 62 percent of firms receiving money from PJSBs are in this category. Loss-making firms report the same level of difficulty in getting a loan from either SOCBs or PJSBs. However, firms with mixed profitability (reporting a loss in one year and profits in another) find it generally easier to get a loan from PJSBs than from SOCBs.

State-owned and joint-stock banks exhibit similar behavior in their lending decisions where size is a criterion. Borrowing from banks exhibits an inverted U-shaped pattern in relation to size. Small companies, both private and state owned, show less tendency to borrow from banks, while firms toward the middle size range show a greater tendency to do so, but then the percentage tapers off among the medium-to-large and large firms. Since 5 percent of private enterprises and 8 percent of SOEs have borrowed both from PJSBs and SOCBs, it is possible to compare access among SOEs and private firms of the same size (table 3.10). The largest difference appears among small firms, where a significantly smaller percentage of private firms than SOEs borrow from SOCBs.

Firms' perceptions about difficulties in obtaining loans from banks (figure 3.8) suggest significant segmentation in the credit market. Private firms and SOEs experience a quite different set of obstacles when trying to access bank loans. For private firms, collateral is by far the main issue, with close to 70 percent of private firms perceiving it as a major problem. Only 14 percent of the SOEs perceive collateral as a binding constraint in their ability to gain access to loans.

The government has been trying to address the collateral issue in part by reforming banking practices and procedures. One step in this

FIGURE 3.8
MAIN DIFFICULTIES IN GETTING BANK LOANS

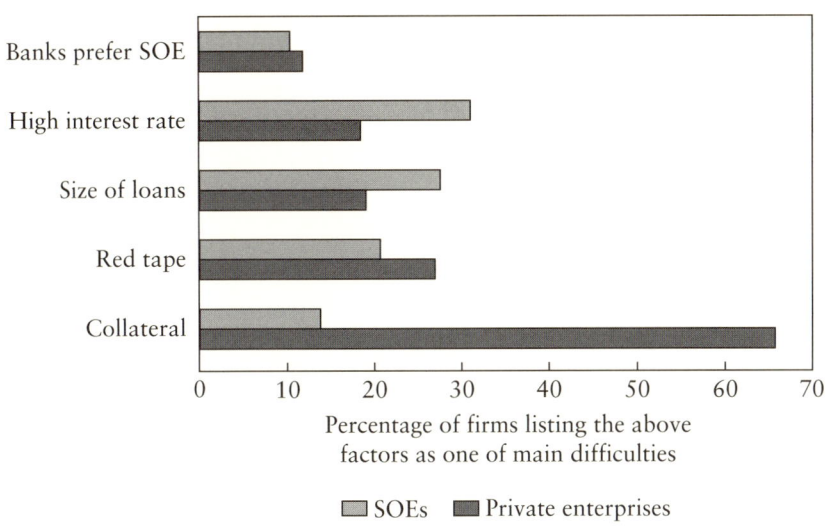

Percentage of firms listing the above
factors as one of main difficulties

☐ SOEs ▪ Private enterprises

SOURCE: Author calculations based on survey data.

direction was Decree 178/1999 ND/CP of December 1999, which allows banks to provide noncollateral loans to their clients. Under this decree, banks are now permitted to give credibility-based loans upon satisfaction of certain requirements. In addition, Decree 178 removes the cap of 70 percent that applied to clients borrowing against their collateral.

Another step has been to review private firms' access to land-use rights, the most popular collateral asset at present. At present, land-use rights can only be accepted as collateral if the clients can provide their "Red Book," that is, the official CLUR.[7] According to a report of the General Department for Land Administration (GDLA), however, up to the beginning of 2002 only 16.8 percent of urban households in Vietnam had been granted CLURs.[8] The CLUR, it should be mentioned, is valued on the basis of an official price band determined

7. To make the system more flexible, the government has ruled that enterprises in the process of obtaining their CLURs will also meet the criteria.

8. *Vietnam Economic Times* website 35 (913) 22-03-2002.

by a provincial price committee. This nonmarket pricing keeps the official price band for land far below the actual market prices and undervalues the collateral.

Apparently the lending practices of commercial banks have not changed much since Decree 178 was put into effect. For private enterprises, collateral remains the most difficult barrier to obtaining bank credit. Furthermore, little has changed in the way collateral is assessed. A number of CEOs stated that the 70 percent upper limit still applies. With the official price band still in place, their assets have been considerably undervalued by the banks' credit officers, and in some extreme cases the maximum amount they can borrow is as low as 10 percent of the market value of their real estate. In view of the size of loans and the system's complicated procedures, many turn to other sources to mobilize capital for their business.

Bank procedures and red tape create further obstacles for private enterprises. About 27 percent of responding CEOs said red tape was one of their major hurdles. Meanwhile, 21 percent of SOEs complained about cumbersome lending procedures, but insufficient size of available loans and high interest rates were also a serious concern. SOEs probably worry more about interest rates and size of loans than private firms do because SOEs are larger firms in general, and hence they tend to demand larger loans. As a stylized fact, SOEs tend to be less efficient than private enterprises. Thus they would have to be at somewhat of a disadvantage compared with private enterprises when facing the same interest rate for borrowings.

Access to Land

The experience of transition countries suggests that the establishment of new property rights in commercial real estate is critical to the growth of the new private sector (Rapaczynski 1996: 96). In Vietnam, the legal framework for land administration has been evolving since the 1998 and 2001 amendments to the Land Law of 1993. Reform in this area needs to continue at an accelerated pace to eliminate the anomalies in the land administration process that are constraining the growth of private enterprises (AusAID 2000).

Land-use rights for commercial use can be obtained in two main ways: through lease from the government and through transfer. The government route is a very long and costly one. At the national level, the GDLA sets the rules and procedures for obtaining CLURs and for leasing and pricing land, and these procedures are supposed to be transparent and the same for state and nonstate enterprises. In reality, however, local official agencies exercised much discretion in approving CLURs, and the procedures could be complicated and lengthy. Private enterprises reported that the average processing time for them was about 200 days, compared with only 2 days for SOEs. Whereas all SOEs reported having to contact one government agency, private entrepreneurs were required to deal with as many as three government agencies. Procedures vary significantly from region to region, however. It is much more difficult for private enterprises to obtain CLURs in Hanoi (average processing time is 325 days), HCMC (418 days), and Da Nang (309 days) than in Bin Duong (64 days) and Hue (82 days).

Furthermore, land in Vietnam is scarce, and any increase in so-called specialized land, which is the category reserved for most business uses, has to come from other categories such as agricultural land. This involves compensation to and resettlement of current users and affects by and large the private firms that typically need new land to enter a sector or to expand their operations.[9] Private enterprises have to pay the compensation costs, which apply not only to the recovered land but also to the assets erected on it, damages to the occupants, and costs relating to any job relocation caused by the clearance process, among others. Since these costs are in addition to the land rental, procuring land-use rights can be a very expensive procedure. Furthermore, disputes often arise over compensation and clearance, and the resulting negotiations can be time-consuming. Thus four to five years can elapse between the application for rights and the time when the land can be put to use by the business. Even so, private businesses are usually required to start paying rents from the date of approval for the leasing. In sum, the process is long and drains away a significant portion of entrepreneurs' resources, thus making it more difficult for them to grow.

Other stipulations apply in the case of land transfer. Land-use rights cannot be transferred without permission of the state. Approval is based on "state planning objectives," allowing for significant administrative discretion. Land users cannot transfer land-use rights without title, the so-called certificate of land-use rights. For

---

9. There is ample evidence that many state enterprises have land in excess of their current needs or expansion plans.

a variety of reasons, however (including complex procedures, high allotment fees, incomplete cadastral mapping, and, more important, few substantive benefits conveyed by land titles in the current environment), a significant percentage of land users do not have CLURs. Furthermore, there is a transfer tax of 2–4 percent. Thus it is not surprising that an estimated 70 percent of all transactions in land-use rights take place in the vibrant unofficial market, where private businesses lease areas of land from SOEs, nonstate enterprises, or directly from households. These unofficial transactions carry substantial risks for business as they are punished by administrative sanctions and therefore cannot serve as a basis for sustained growth.

Findings from our survey confirm the prevalence of informal transactions in land-use rights. As figure 3.9 shows, about half of the sample firms have been granted land-use rights (for residential purposes), and a majority of them are small-scale businesses. Of these, about 13 percent of the private companies do not have a CLUR. For historical and other reasons, many private firms and individual or family-based businesses do not hold CLURs, although there is an incentive for private enterprises to seek CLURs as a basis for securing finance from banks. At the same time, many small, family-based businesses in the sample prefer not to have CLURs because of the

FIGURE 3.9
PRIVATE FIRMS' MAIN PREMISES

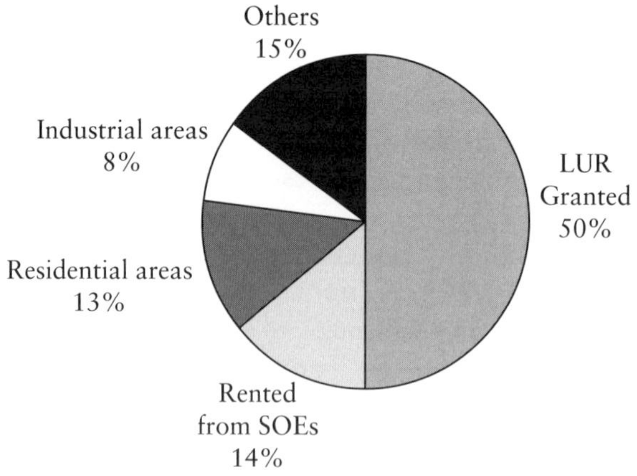

SOURCE: Author calculations based on survey data.

68

perception that they were not likely to receive formal bank lending anyway. Moreover, they would have to pay annual fees by holding these rights. This is an important disincentive to formalizing land-use rights.

About 14 percent of respondents had obtained access to land by leasing from SOEs, 13 percent had leased from households in residential areas, and 8 percent had leased in industrial areas. Private enterprises typically have to pay the prevailing market prices for leasing land from SOEs. Obtaining land-use rights in industrial zones and areas is treated as part of the formal market. Although a relatively low proportion of sample firms have land in industrial areas, these areas, especially in the big cities, are becoming increasingly important ways of providing land for private enterprises. In recent years, People's Committees in provinces surrounding the major cities have come to realize that attracting more private enterprises can help stimulate the local economy (JBIC 2002). Hence they have been pushing to provide more land-use rights to private enterprises, many of them in the cities' industrial areas. Private enterprises in our sample had received no assigned land from the state for commercial uses.

Table 3.11 reports the share of sample firms that had obtained CLURs and those that were still in the process of applying for them. Overall, the majority of sample firms have received CLURs. A significantly larger proportion of private enterprises compared with state enterprises do not have CLURs.

The social cost of the existing anomalies in the area of land-use rights is potentially very high, as access to land appears to be a major factor enabling business expansion. When asked how one's business would change if land were easier or cheaper to obtain, 82 percent of CEOs said they would expand plant size, and about one-third said they would diversify into new activities (table 3.12). Interestingly,

TABLE 3.11
POSSESSION OF CLURs BY SAMPLE FIRMS
(percent of total)

Enterprise	No	Yes	In application
Private	31	62	7
SOE	18	70	12

SOURCE: Author calculations based on survey data.

TABLE 3.12
CEOs' Choices If Land Available
(percent of total)

Choice	No	Yes	Missing	Total[a]
No change	87	6	7	100 (225)
Expand plant size	12	82	6	100 (225)
Diversify into new activities	59	35	6	100 (225)
Reduce dependency on SOEs	87	7	6	100 (225)

a. Number of observations in parentheses.
SOURCE: Author calculations based on survey data.

difficult access to land does not seem to create or exacerbate private firms' dependence on SOEs.

Performance

As already noted, our analysis has revealed significant segmentation in the business sector and in the business environment. To assess the situation with regard to business performance, we look at two indicators of performance: growth in labor employed by sample firms and rate of return on assets. The employment indicator is a more reliable indicator of market performance.[10]

As research has established, entrants' profits in successful transition economies follow a distinct path. Initially, new firms earn very high profits as they enter into unfilled market niches in typically very distorted economies. As high profits attract more entrants, profits tend to converge to more normal levels. In China at the start of reforms in 1979, for example, the average profits of nonstate firms were 28 percent of invested capital. As China's transition proceeded, the new firms' profits declined steadily through the first decade of

---

10. Data on the financial performance of Vietnamese enterprises should be interpreted with caution. Enterprises have an incentive to misrepresent their financial results and scale of operations. Since many SOEs are overstaffed, any movements in their employment levels are not necessarily in response to market signals. Furthermore, many asset prices, prices of land-use rights in particular, are not market based, especially for state-owned enterprises. For these reasons, trends in performance are more reliable than absolute levels.

reform, falling to 15 percent of invested capital in 1984 and leveling out at 6 percent in 1991 (Naughton 1995: 150). Similarly, profit rates of manufacturing firms in Poland in their first year of operation fell from an average of 25 percent of invested capital for firms formed in 1990 to 6 percent for firms formed in 1995. Small businesses in the United States typically earn returns between 9 and 15 percent of assets. Thus the time pattern of performance, particularly the degree of convergence to a "normal" level, is an important indicator of the success of reforms (McMillan and Woodruff 2002).

Since 1999, the average private firm in our sample has experienced a decline in both employment growth and return on assets (see figures 3.10 and 3.11). The opposite is the case among state-owned firms in the sample: their performance is in general worse than that of private firms but is showing some improvement and convergence toward private firm levels. Several factors may account for the divergent trends in the performance of these enterprises. The decline in rates of employment growth and return on assets in the case of private firms coincides with the dramatic rise in new registrations and increased competition among private firms following the implementation of the new Enterprise Law. Competition from new entrants is

FIGURE 3.10
ANNUAL GROWTH IN NUMBER OF EMPLOYEES BY ENTERPRISE TYPE

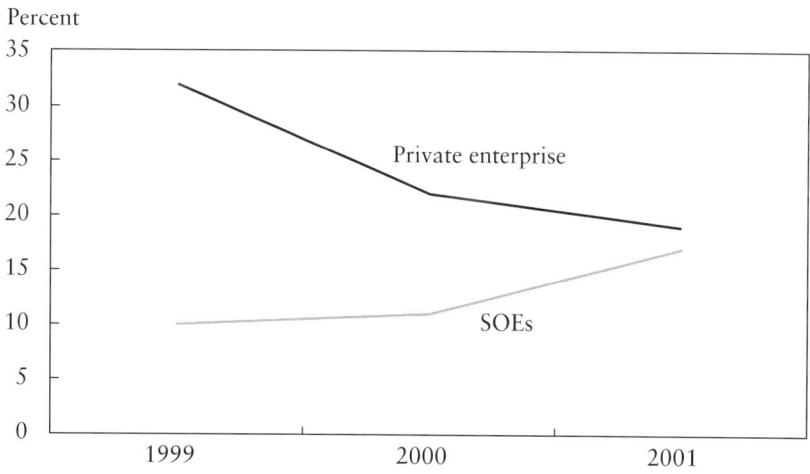

SOURCE: Author calculations based on survey data.

FIGURE 3.11

ANNUAL RETURN ON TOTAL ASSETS BY ENTERPRISE TYPE

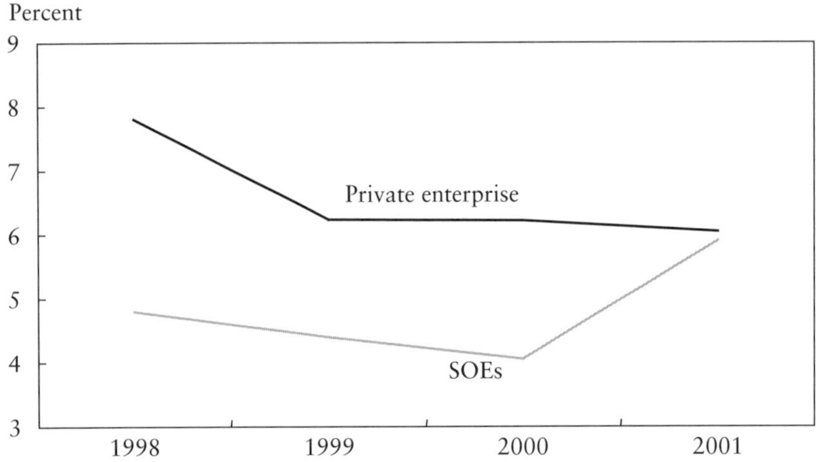

SOURCE: Author calculations based on survey data.

more likely to affect the private firms that are more heavily represented in sectors with relatively low barriers to entry.

The period since 1999 also reflects the effects of the regional recovery from the Asian crisis. The impact of the recovery process is being felt by both types of enterprises but is perhaps more pronounced among SOEs, which are somewhat better protected from competition from new entry.

Finally, improvements in SOE performance may indicate adjustments to market signals. In recent years, Vietnam has seen the emergence of new state business interests whereby many state-owned enterprises have adapted quite successfully to the market economy. As Oxford Analytica (2002) points out, the picture of a universally ailing state sector is misleading.

A similar negative correlation between the performance of private and state-owned firms has been observed in China with respect to the behavior of earnings before interest and taxes and returns on equity (Chan 2002: 37). According to Chan, this is most likely related to the fact that private enterprises are concentrated in downstream industries where they usually lack pricing power, whereas SOEs are concentrated in the heavy industrial commodities sector. Therefore strong commodity prices tend to benefit SOEs but to adversely affect private industrial enterprises, and vice versa.

Profitability of domestic private firms in our sample correlates positively with their main customers being Vietnamese individuals and negatively with their main customers being other private firms. It correlates strongly positively and significantly with local governments being the main customer. For SOEs, profit margins are positively but statistically insignificantly correlated with foreign companies being the main customer. When asked how a firm was doing in terms of general growth, 83 percent of the private CEOs said their businesses were growing, 14 percent said the businesses remained the same, and only 3 percent of the CEOs said they were downsizing their businesses. We find that the level of formality as reflected in firms' reliance on the banking system when conducting business transactions and in the share of workers with formal labor contracts is not significantly associated with firms' performance.

Conclusion

Sample firms provided important information on some key aspects of their business environment, most notably, the competition and access to financing, land, and business services. We found, for example, no strong direct relationship between degree of informality and a firm's ability to access resources such as bank loans, land, business services, and the court system. At the same time, a significant degree of segmentation exists in the business environment with respect to the same firm characteristics that we found to be important in the case of informality, namely, ownership and size.

State-owned and private enterprises differ significantly in terms of their main customers, suppliers, and competitors. Private firms show greater dependence on social networks for access to market, capital, and business services, but their business networks are weaker than is the case for state-owned enterprises. A comparison of the sources of financing for private firms and SOEs provides evidence of the segmented nature of the financial market in Vietnam. Different factors act as determinants of bank borrowing for private versus state-owned enterprises. Profitability and size in particular are positively associated with bank borrowing among private enterprises, but not among state-owned enterprises. Major anomalies exist in the area of land-use rights, which seem to have a particularly negative impact on the growth of private firms. The observed segmentation in the business sector and the business environment finds a corresponding pattern in business performance. A decline occurs in both employment growth and return on assets for private firms. This trend coincides with the rapid growth of new registrations and increased competition among private firms. The opposite trend is observed among state-owned firms, whose performance is in general worse than that of private firms but is showing some improvement and convergence toward the levels attained by private firms. The observed patterns of private firm performance underscore the importance of improving the business environment to expand the opportunities for private companies to grow and develop. Without a conducive environment, the reported numbers on rates of return for private firms may be too low to sustain the robust creation of new businesses.

Appendix

TABLE 3.13
RESORT TO THE LEGAL SYSTEM

Variables	Coefficient	Standard error	P-value
Intercept	–17.5	17.7	0.32
Ownership dummy (1 is private)	–0.06	0.07	0.42
Number of business disputes*	13.4	4.9	0.007
Customers within city*	0.17	0.08	0.035
Size (log of number of employees in 2001* (number of employees)	0.03	0.008	0.000
Business network strength	–1.34	4.3	0.75
Arrears as percentage of sales	0.03	0.1	0.80
Strength of social network (friends-family)	1.2	0.9	0.19
Number of observations	70		
R-square	0.33		

*Statistically significant at the 5 percent level.
NOTE: Dependent variable is percentage of disputes brought to court.
SOURCE: Author calculations based on survey data.

TABLE 3.14
Determinants of Importance of Bank Loans in Firm Financing

	SOEs				Private				Pooled sample			
	(1)	(2)	(3)	(4)	(1)	(2)	(3)	(4)	(1)	(2)	(3)	(4)
Constant	6.3	27.5*	23.4*	13.1	–2.8	9.1*	8.2*	–3.9	7.5	27*	24*	11
	(21)	(4.8)	(4.5)	(24.5)	(4.0)	(1.5)	(2)	(5)	(7)	(3.1)	(2.8)	(8.5)
Size	3.34			2.9	3.06*			2.8*	3.1*			2.8*
	(3.7)			(4.3)	(1.0)			(1.2)	(1.1)			(1.4)
Profitability(gross profit margin)		–21.2		–28.7		1.03*		1.0*		1.0*		1*
		(46.2)		(48)		(0.3)		(0.2)		(0.3)		(0.3)
CLUR			3.9	–3.00			1.9	3.9			2.4	2.1
			(8.1)	(10)			(2.7)	(3.2)			(2.9)	(3.7)
Ownership dummy (1 is private)									–11*	–18*	–16*	–14*
									(3.8)	(3.7)	(3.2)	(4.5)
Number of observations	55	48	60	45	129	111	150	100	185	160	211	146
R-square	0.02	0.01	0.00	0.02	0.07	0.14	0.00	0.21	0.14	0.16	0.1	0.19

*Statistically significant at the 1 percent level.
NOTE: Dependent variable is share of bank loans in total financing. CLUR is certificate of land-use rights. Standard errors in parentheses.
SOURCE: Author calculations based on survey data.

4

Reducing Regulatory Burdens and Leveling the Playing Field

Higher regulatory burdens and arbitrary and capricious applications of rules and regulations contribute to informality. Systematic biases in the business environment also create incentives for higher informality as a way to compensate for an uneven playing field. High levels of informality are socially costly. They are indicative of an environment in which rules and regulations are not binding and are therefore ineffective as tools of government policy. Informality also has direct and indirect costs for businesses. In the intermediate forms of informality, where businesses interact with the government but do not fully comply with regulations, direct costs such as camouflaging noncompliance and paying a higher corruption tax can outweigh the indirect costs related to the loss in capacity to benefit from participation in regulated markets and activities. By contrast, enterprises that are completely outside the formal system tend to incur higher indirect costs but are typically able to minimize or eliminate direct regulatory burdens. Although informality tends to compensate to some extent for systematic biases in the business environment, it does not eliminate the distortions in the allocation of resources associated with an uneven playing field. Thus the society as a whole will benefit from a higher degree of formality as a result of reducing excessive regulatory burdens, making reasonable laws and regulations more enforceable, and leveling the playing field.

Toward More Enforceable Laws and Regulations

To make laws and regulations more enforceable will require changes both in the nature of the laws and regulations and in the enforcement process. First and foremost, laws and regulations need to be reasonable. Those that run against the interests of almost everyone in society are almost impossible to enforce, or they can be enforced only at the expense of the legitimacy of the government. Second, the enforcement process needs to utilize to some extent the energy of incentives and interests of parties that are likely to benefit from the enforcement of rules and regulations.

Making Regulations More Reasonable and Consistent. The current regulatory framework in Vietnam contains numerous biases against growth, particularly the growth of private firms. Larger firms are inspected more, and higher returns are taxed punitively. Certain types of expenditures that are particularly important for creating and exploiting market opportunities, such as marketing expenses, are not tax-exempt above the cap. These measures encourage informality and penalize growth. Indeed, private enterprises operate with a high level of informality in Vietnam. Their behavior reflects the belief that the costs of higher visibility in the form of larger size or more transparency outweigh the benefits, because larger size and higher transparency invite inspections and bureaucratic harassment. Such administrative biases against size and growth need to be abolished. Regulations should not run against the logic of normal business practices. To maintain the rapid growth of the private sector, an environment supportive of transforming SMEs into larger enterprises needs to be established.

Entrepreneurs often complain about inconsistent and conflicting laws and regulations. Vietnam has many such laws and regulations in force at present, and they complicate the enforcement process, especially because they encourage subjective interpretations. For example, Decree No. 52/1999/ND-CP and Decree No. 12/2000/ND-CP require investors applying for land-use rights to attach a business plan that has been approved as part of their business registration. There is, however, no competent authority to issue such approval because, pursuant to new regulations, business projects of private investors are not necessarily examined and approved by the State (Nguyen Dinh Tai 2002).

Inconsistencies are often present within the same law. For example, the 1998 Law on Complaints lays out a path for appeals of local administrative decisions. At the same time, it requires complainants to accept the findings of the relevant body without appeal (Quinn 2002). The inconsistencies between laws and regulations are exacerbated by the fact that a large number of laws and regulations periodically enter, but few if any exit, the legal domain. To avoid confusion, new and amended laws should supersede existing old laws completely, and not only in case of conflict between the new and the old law.

The approval and licensing spirit still permeates many laws and regulations. This takes the form of attempts to be specific and detailed in proscribing behavior. Although in certain cases very detailed specificity in the law can be highly desirable, more often than not it actually increases bureaucratic discretion or the delays in implementation. The practice of waiting for detailed implementing regulations after a law has been passed reflects such an administrative culture. For example, seven months elapsed between the promulgation of the Enterprise Law and the issuance of the first implementing regulations. Similarly with the Labor Code, many months elapsed before the appearance of any implementing regulations. This kind of behavior leads to inaction at the local level, leaving local governments paralyzed as they wait for implementing regulations to be developed and handed to them.

The production of implementing regulations in Vietnam is complicated by the perceived need to make a positive mention of every eventuality in the law and by the fact that if it is not mentioned, then that activity is prohibited. The end result is a large number of implementing regulations and frequent changes in these regulations, as regulators always discover that they have missed something. For example, there are currently about 500 implementing guidelines for the Land Law (Cao Minh Truc 2002). Often by the time the new law is promulgated, it is already in need of revision, as it cannot explicitly accommodate newly emerging business needs. Entrepreneurs need to see revisions in the Labor Code and the standard labor contract, for instance, to accommodate newly developed industries such as insurance agents. In line with the new amendments to Vietnam's Constitution, it has been recommended that the government move from a "positive list" to a "negative list" approach so that activities not mentioned as being prohibited under the law are automatically permitted (Tran Phuong Binh 2002).

Furthermore, the practice of using rigid contract forms for important business transactions such as labor contracts, lease of land-use rights, and the like reflects an interfering attitude by the state aimed at managing and controlling private transactions. Such an attitude restricts the number of alternatives available to private parties and results in suboptimal arrangements. It also encourages informality and makes businesses vulnerable to bureaucratic discretion. Some contract forms fail to take into account the normal interests of the contracting parties. For example, the Labor Law and the labor contract form do not spell out obligations of the employees to the employers and fail to recognize the interest of the enterprise in this reciprocal relationship.

Policymakers need to focus on developing an even more transparent and consistent framework for private sector development based on the rule of law. They need to foster a more even playing field and reduce the costs of complying with rules and regulations. Informal activities should gradually be absorbed into the formal market system by simplifying rules and regulations and by better enforcing and protecting property rights. The shift from concessionary (known as asking-giving in Vietnam) to normative regulations, as demonstrated by the passage and implementation of the Enterprise Law, should be extended to other areas, land-use rights in particular. Policymakers also need to introduce greater fairness, transparency, and consistency in the taxation of private firms. Tax provisions that are inconsistent with normal business practices and penalize growth should be abolished. Taxation policies should be such that people are not forced to hide what they have earned in an honest way. The creation of a vibrant private sector depends to a large extent on the level of confidence that private investors have in the system and how much they believe that the rules do not discriminate against them and that enforcement is fair.

How can this shift from a complicated and inconsistent legal framework to a simpler and transparent one be achieved? The legal needs assessment provides a comprehensive platform for developing a long-term prioritized strategy for improving the overall legal framework (Government of Vietnam 2001). Implementation has already begun. It is of concern, however, that state administrative bodies in Vietnam have little interest in finding and amending inconsistent and costly regulations in order to improve the business environment. The working culture of government agencies now seems to be focused on protecting and enhancing their own rights and interests, while leaving difficulties in compliance and interpretation to market participants or other agencies at local levels, for example (CIEM 2002). It should become a routine practice of regulatory agencies to periodically review regulations from the point of view of their efficiency and enforceability. Regulations that have outlived their usefulness or relevance should be retired from the system.

Supporting Enforcement with Market Incentives. A high degree of informality is typically associated with low credibility about government capacity and its commitment to the implementation of new laws and regulations. The policy shift from high informality to better enforcement should take this into account and include measures that enhance the capacity of the government to precommit itself in order to build trust. Such measures should ultimately be based on the incentives of the affected parties. For example, increasing enterprises' reliance on the banking system should be in the interest of the banking community. Reducing fees related to banking transactions and enhancing the range of services that banks offer their clients will create incentives to open more bank accounts. At present, the low number of bank accounts in Vietnam in relation to the population reflects an element of distrust in the government and in the banking system. Box 4.1 describes China's approach to enhancing private actors' trust in the government through the transitional institution of anonymous banking.[1] The practice has proved very effective in increasing savings in China and in monetizing the economy (Bai and others 1999).[2]

Similarly, enforcing labor regulations in the area of nonwage compensation should theoretically be in the interest of the workers. In practice, however, workers tend to adopt a short-term outlook and prefer higher take-home pay to paying their contributions. Belser

---

1. Government Decree 70 dated November 21, 2000, and Circular 02 of the State Bank of Vietnam dated April 4, 2001, provide specific regulations on bank confidentiality in Vietnam. Banks are prohibited from disclosing information relating to deposits or assets of customers to third parties, except where expressly agreed by their customers, where requested by competent state bodies, or where necessary in support of their internal activities. Internal bank regulations for compliance with confidentiality obligations and archiving of minutes for every case of disclosure are mandatory. Sanctions for confidentiality breaches include a warning, fine, or criminal prosecution.

2. As Qian (2001) emphasizes, "The institution of anonymous banking is not only unconventional but also against the recommended principle of transparency. But it has an economic logic: when other institutional means are not working, it serves as a commitment device to limiting government predation by reducing the amount of information available to it. The government accepts such a constraint because it benefits from the revenue out of the banking system through its control over interest rate and capital flow. Although such a practice of financial repression is against the usual policy recommendations, it plays a crucial role in inducing the government to give up discretionary taxes on individuals."

BOX 4.1
CHINA'S TRANSITIONAL INSTITUTIONS FOR REDUCING ARBITRARY
GOVERNMENT INTRUSION INTO ECONOMIC ACTIVITIES:
CASH TRANSACTIONS AND ANONYMOUS BANKING

In pre-reform China, private entrepreneurs and rural households often had to contend with state predation and a continuous streak of broken government promises. The reform unleashed enormous private incentives that fueled rapid economic growth despite the absence of conventional institutions of law to constrain the government from arbitrary intrusion into economic activities. According to Bai and others (1999), two mechanisms that have limited the government's predation and harassment are cash transactions and anonymous banking.

Over a period of time, the government gradually but significantly loosened its control over the use of cash. As a result, cash in circulation in the economy steadily increased, from less than 6 percent in 1978 to a peak of 17 percent in 1993. In recent years it has leveled off to about 13 percent.

As early as 1950, the Chinese government formulated "four principles" to encourage private savings in state banks: voluntary deposit, free withdrawal, the bearing of interest, and confidentiality. The confidentiality principle stated that the banks had an obligation to "keep depositors secret."

These principles were restated in the revised regulations of 1980 and 1992, which allowed individuals to open savings accounts without personal identification. They also allowed individuals to freely choose types of deposits, either "named" or "unnamed." The effect of anonymous household bank deposits on the economy was very limited before the reform, since household income was low and private activities were virtually banned. After the reform, private business became legal, and the state loosened its control over cash and oversight over transactions. Every individual, including the newly rich, could use anonymous bank deposits as a safe haven to store his or her wealth. Many businesses also opened bank accounts under false household names, illegally but quite safely, because it was difficult to catch and prosecute the holders. The policy of anonymous banking has contributed significantly to the growth of savings and to the financial deepening and monetization of the economy. Some influential Chinese scholars and deputies of the National People's Congress have reportedly advocated abandoning anonymous bank deposits, arguing that they contribute to pervasive corruption, tax evasion, and money laundering, especially by the newly rich. The central bank seriously considered and rejected such proposals several times. Finally, in 2000, China abandoned anonymous banking, but by then the credibility of the government and its capacity to commit itself not to intrude on private businesses and households had been firmly established.

SOURCE: Bai and others (1999).

(2000) attributes this behavior to the fact that pensions are not adjusted for inflation, and to the low level of workers' confidence in Vietnam's new social security institutions. Workers tend to perceive nonwage benefits as a tax rather than as an insurance against risk. Changing these perceptions and increasing workers' confidence in the new social security system are therefore necessary steps toward greater compliance with labor regulations.

To increase confidence and economize on resources, the government should rely more on indirect control in enforcing increasingly complex regulations. Although the tendency among individual entrepreneurs is normally to free-ride with respect to compliance, it is often in the collective interests of entrepreneurs that regulations be enforced. Business associations as instruments of collective actions can internalize the public benefits associated with regulations and taxation. They can therefore play an important role in introducing a higher degree of formality.

There are about 200 business associations in Vietnam, and membership in them is growing. Most are sectoral or regional associations. Of the country's six national umbrella or peak associations, the Vietnam Chamber of Commerce and Industry (VCCI) is the largest and most established. Some of these associations have been active in representing business interests before the government. Certain regulations require ministers to solicit comments from business associations before promulgating new legal documents related to business activities.[3] VCCI, for example, had an active part in drafting the Enterprise Law and has commented on other important laws and regulations.

Despite their rapid growth, business associations are somewhat limited in what they can do today to promote the interest of the business community. Furthermore, the legal and regulatory regime for establishing an association is confusing. The government is preparing a Law on Associations, which is expected to improve the regime for establishing an association. The business associations themselves insist that establishing such an organization should be as easy as and similar to establishing an enterprise under the Enterprise Law (Nguyen and Stromseth 2002).

If business associations are to play a meaningful role and have the credibility they need with their members, they must be perceived

---

3. Decision No. 310 TTg and Directive No. 16/1998/CT0-TTg.

as being independent from the government and as truly representing the interests of their members. Some associations in Vietnam are still viewed as extensions of the government and continue to receive significant financial support from it. This is creating an uneven playing field and in the long run does little to help these institutions represent business interests.

The government should create an environment that makes it possible for business associations to become financially independent. Associations currently in existence do not receive the standard privileges connected with the public good (or club good) nature of the services they provide, such as tax exemptions on income from core activities and tax deductions for dues paid by members. Many business services, such as trade and investment promotion activities, are provided mainly by state agencies, although business associations are in many ways in a better position to do so. These constraints are preventing some of them from expanding and gaining legitimacy with existing or potential members. The government should authorize business associations to carry out some tasks and projects of a public service nature such as providing business support services, issuing professional training certificates, and conducting business registration. Some should also be allowed to engage in self-regulation by adopting and enforcing professional standards of conduct. Business associations, however, should not be allowed to become instruments in the hands of incumbents for restricting market access.

Improving Accountability and Incentives within the Bureaucracy. A high degree of informality typically reflects a combination of excessive regulations, poor enforcement capacity, and low government credibility. Implementation capacity and commitment to reform can be enhanced by administrative reforms. In the present administrative system in Vietnam, many government agencies that have important interactions with the business community have overlapping responsibilities and lack clear accountability. This often results in slow administrative decisionmaking. Measures to clarify roles and responsibilities within the bureaucracy would greatly improve government business interactions. The adoption of the Public Administration Reform Master Program in September 2001 is an important reform measure and is expected to address these issues. One of the strategic objectives of PAR is to improve the delivery of administrative services to the people at the provincial, municipal/district, and commune/ward level. As indicated by the Swiss Agency for Development and Cooperation and Government Committee for Organization and Personnel of Vietnam (Do 2002), there have been significant improvements in administrative service delivery in recent years. Under the heading "one door" or "one-stop shop" (OSS), administrative services in many provinces, cities, and rural districts have improved significantly in terms of accessibility, transparency, effectiveness, and efficiency. In addition, the time spent on processing administrative services has been reduced dramatically in certain localities, particularly in the case of land contract transfers and certificates of land-use rights (box 4.2). Thus it seems that there is much to gain, especially at the administrative district level, from establishing the typical model of OSS service delivery.

To increase accountability, government officials should pay more attention to the rights of citizens and entrepreneurs. Entrepreneurs often complain about the tendency of officials in certain localities to stop licensing businesses that are deemed "sensitive" by the local authorities. These may include karaoke, hairdressing parlors, and the like. Sometimes officials tend to substitute for the market in deciding whether the business that an entrepreneur wants to register is needed given the number of already established enterprises of a similar kind (CIEM 2003). Businessmen should have sufficient protection against arbitrary abuses of administrative authority in areas such as illegal layoffs, issuance of licenses, illegal assessment of taxes and fees, and land use.

The creation of the Administrative Courts in 1995, the promulgation of the Civil Code in 1996, and the 1998 Law on Complaints and Denunciations, along with the 1998 amended Ordinance on Procedures for Resolving Administrative Cases, provided the public with avenues to obtaining redress and mediation in disputes with government administrators. It has now become accepted that state agencies can be sued in the courts. The administrative courts deal with complaints about official abuse and corruption.

However, the citizens and economic subjects of Vietnam do not have an effective system of recourse against abuses of administrative power. Of the 140,782 cases heard by the courts in Vietnam in 2000, only 333 were in the administrative courts (Quinn 2002).[4] The chief

---

4. By comparison, the Philippine Office of Management and Budget reported more than 3,000 new administrative cases in 2001.

BOX 4.2
INCREASED EFFICIENCY OF "ONE-STOP-SHOP"
DELIVERY IN NHOA QUAN DISTRICT

With the introduction of OSS service delivery, efficiency has increased in all OSSs evaluated in 2002 by the Swiss Agency for Development and Cooperation and Government Committee for Organization and Personnel of Vietnam. In all cases, a smaller staff is now able to handle more services in less time. In Nho Quan District, as in all OSSs visited, significantly less time was spent on each service request as a direct result of introducing OSS service delivery.

SERVICE EFFICIENCY GAINS IN NHO QUAHN

	Time to solve a case	
Service	Before OSS	After OSS
Land contract transfers (days)	28	20
Certificate of land-use right (days)	13	7
Notarization (minutes)	10	7
Business registration (days)	7	5

A simple calculation shows the amount of money Nho Quan District saved in land administration (in the handling of land contract transfers and certifying land-use rights) by introducing land administration services in the OSS. With one staff member earning VND 15,000 a day and with the equivalent of one staff member working a quarter of his total time on solving one particular case, the saving on a land contract transfer can be VND 30,000, and on certifying a land-use right it can be VND 26,250. Assuming that on an annual basis, 300 land contract transfers and 500 certifications of land-use rights take place, that adds up to an annual cost saving of VND 22,125,000 (US$1,475). And that is just one service area. Nhoa Quan District is saving significant sums of money now that services are provided through the OSS. Similar results have been recorded in all other OSSs visited. In larger OSSs, the potential cost savings through efficiency gains are likely to be even higher owing to economies of scale.

SOURCE: Do and others (2002).

judge of the Supreme Court noted in his report to the National Assembly that the number of administrative cases currently being heard does not reflect the true demand for the administrative courts. Rather, burdensome filing requirements tend to act as a filter to prevent large numbers of cases from being accepted by the administrative courts for hearing, as indicated by the discrepancy between the number of complaints and administrative suits. In 2001, for example, 3,619 complaints were reported, whereas only 453 cases were filed. This shows that the barriers to entry in the administrative courts remain a major problem.

Statistics also show (Quinn 2002) that the backlog for administrative cases is much higher than for any other types of cases: only one-third of administrative cases received were categorized as completed, versus more than 50 percent of all other cases. Several factors may contribute to the lower effectiveness of administrative courts. Inconsistencies between various laws and regulations give judges the discretion to refuse to hear administrative cases.[5] The important role that local governments play in personnel and budgetary matters of the courts makes provincial courts dependent on the local authorities.[6] Hence it is unrealistic to expect an unbiased outcome in administrative suits. Finally, there are serious conflicts of interest in the way administrative complaints are handled. Local authorities that are responsible for the problem in the first place also act as arbitrators of the complaint process. Complainants are therefore less likely to have positive outcomes.

To provide entrepreneurs with effective protection against administrative abuse, these issues need to be addressed. Inconsistencies between laws need to be eliminated to reduce bureaucratic discretion. The filing process needs to be simplified and made less costly for citizens in order to reduce the barriers to entry into the administrative process. Conflicts of interest need to be eliminated by ensuring that judges and arbitrators are independent from offenders.

---

5. For example, the Law on Complaints requires that a citizen pursue all complaints about government action internally within the administrative bureaucracy and not within the courts. The Amended Ordinance on Procedures for Resolving Administrative Disputes, on the other hand, allows cases to enter the courts without having exhausted all internal appeals (Quinn 2002).

6. Judges are limited to five-year terms. Through the reappointment process, the local political establishment has leverage to indirectly influence judges. Budgeting for the Provincial People's Court is undertaken by the local Departments of Justice through the provincial governments. Provincial courts rely on local governments for access to the financial resources required to undertake day-to-day operations. As a result, they are sensitive to the concerns of local governments (Quinn 2002).

It is also important to create stronger positive incentives within the bureaucracy that reward success in promoting broadly based development. Officials who are responsible for administration of the economy should be well trained and paid wages that motivate them to work in the interest of the community. Official wages should not be at levels that imply that bribes and corruption are factored in. It has been estimated that unofficial income accounts for about 50 percent of the official income of government employees (Phan 2001). The government has developed plans to have a smaller administrative apparatus staffed by professionally qualified, motivated, and well-paid officials. Box 4.3 describes the experience with government reforms in Shunde, a city in China's Guangdong Province.

From a systemic point of view, many businessmen believe that corruption is perhaps the single largest threat to social stability and economic development in Vietnam. The repeated prosecution of big corruption cases is likely to go some way toward reducing the problem, particularly if the authorities continue to impose stiff penalties for such offenses. Nevertheless, a dramatic reduction in corruption will not occur without broader structural change. The notion that public office should carry private benefits as a matter of right remains widespread. Officials do not view the receipt of small amounts of money for carrying out bureaucratic functions as corruption. Preliminary steps have been taken in this regard insofar as recent regulations and legislation seek to distinguish between "public" and "private" by requiring officials to declare their assets as well as setting out what constitute conflicts of interest in relation to officials' (and their families') business activities. This is a new concept, however, and is poorly enforced. Increases in civil service salaries—scheduled to occur as public sector employment falls—may go some way toward encouraging this ethos. In some countries, an independent agency with the authority to fight corruption has been necessary to reform the administrative apparatus effectively, a prime example being the Independent Commission against Corruption in Hong Kong.

Leveling the Playing Field

An uneven playing field is fertile ground for informality. Although Vietnam has made significant progress toward creating a more level playing field, the business environment still harbors systematic biases against small and medium private enterprises. If these biases are to be

BOX 4.3

LOCAL GOVERNMENT REFORM IN SHUNDE,
GUANGDONG PROVINCE, CHINA

Located on the Pearl River Delta in China's Guangdong Province, Shunde is a new city of about 1.2 million people. Government reform in Shunde started in 1993 and was a radical exercise by any measure. It reduced the number of government agencies by nearly half and the number of employees by 40 percent, transformed the functions of the government, increased the transparency of government administration, and enhanced the rule of law. Reform in Shunde was closely linked with the privatization of state-owned enterprises under the city's jurisdiction. In effect, the ownership transformation provided the conditions for government reform. Shunde's leadership played an indispensable role in bringing about the government reform. Under the influence of the party secretary, the entire leadership adopted a new philosophy toward government administration: that is, the government endeavored to draw away from direct engagement in the economic affairs and to concentrate instead on public good provision (including the provision of a fair, just, and open competitive environment) and law implementation.

A factor contributing to Shunde's success is its well-designed reform plan. Laid-off workers were not simply released from the government. Instead, they were first put into government-supported companies in the transition period. Subsequently, these companies were privatized, and the workers were gradually absorbed by the private sector. The downsizing met with resistance not only from those who lost their government jobs but also from the higher level of government. It is standard practice in China for lower-level governments to have the same, if not more, departments than a higher level of government. The elimination and consolidation of departments in Shunde thus created the potential for conflict with Guangdong's provincial government. This problem was solved, however, by letting each remaining department assume more responsibilities and by considerably increasing the workload of the remaining employees. This was associated with a significant wage increase for the remaining government employees. The government has also established a "one-stop shop" for administrative services and has transformed arbitrary administrative fees into stable local taxes, which have reduced corruption. A related development is that the city has seen a sharp increase in foreign direct investment.

SOURCE: Yao (2000).

eliminated, the SOE sector will require deeper reform, and private firms should have greater access to capital and land.

Establishing a Level Playing Field for SOEs and Private Businesses. An important indirect social cost associated with state ownership is that it encourages what the private sector considers to be excessive government intervention. State enterprises that have weak incentives and are somewhat insulated from competition through direct and indirect subsidies can tolerate higher tax rates and more intense government intervention than private enterprises. In this way, significant state ownership encourages excessive government intervention in the economy. Reducing state ownership is therefore an important condition for creating a more efficient regulatory environment.

However, the Vietnamese authorities intend to retain a sizable number of SOEs under state control. To ensure that the playing field is more level for both state-owned and private businesses, the authorities will therefore need to pay special attention to three aspects of enterprise reform: SOE corporatization, ownership diversification, and the management of state assets. Such reforms will in turn accelerate the process of equitization, since many equitized companies complain that they begin to experience problems as soon as they sever their links with the government.

To unify the treatment of state-owned and nonstate enterprises, it is necessary to corporatize state-owned enterprises and bring them under the Enterprise Law. Corporatized SOEs would be superior to uncorporatized ones in terms of alleviating administrative interference, enhancing managerial autonomy, and improving enterprise performance. With corporatization, issues of corporate governance would assume practical relevance. The corporate form would create some of the internal mechanisms for the exercise of corporate control, such as a board of directors, control boards, and shareholder meetings. But significant institution building needs to take place as well, to create the mechanisms that corporate governance calls for, particularly external mechanisms such as institutional investors, bankruptcy legislation, credit-rating agencies, and bureaus.

The conversion of SOEs into limited liability companies (LLCs) would not change ownership rights, but it would affect the way these rights are exercised. The success of such conversion depends greatly on who is assigned ownership rights and how the specified owner chooses to exercise those rights. If LLCs are to be operated as commercial, market-oriented, and profit-maximizing entities, then the bodies assuming ownership and corporate governance functions over the LLCs must themselves be commercialized entities with hard budget constraints seeking to maximize the performance of the LLCs.

Corporatization and the establishment of a commercially oriented state ownership agency (see box 4.4) would facilitate ownership diversification. Corporatization and the limited liability form would make it feasible and perhaps economically attractive to draw in non-state capital. In addition, outside investors could facilitate the management of state assets, as they would add an independent outside source of market monitoring.

China's experience with SOE reform offers valuable lessons for Vietnam, especially for its general corporations, which can be compared with the enterprise group in China. Beijing is attempting to simplify the organizational framework of these groups, to reorient them toward managing financial rather than administrative assets, to introduce independent professional managers, and to increase outsider participation. Another important task is to de-link their social and commercial functions.

Also instructive is China's experience in building the mechanisms of modern corporate governance (Tenev and Zhang 2002). The driving force in this area has been the Chinese Securities and Exchange Commission, whose objective is to protect the minority shareholders of listed SOEs. China has also established a specialized agency for the management of state assets. These and other aspects of China's experiments in enterprise reform should help Vietnam design its own reforms with a "follower's advantage" (Oxford Analytica 2002).

Improving Private Enterprises' Access to Finance. State-owned enterprise reform,[7] particularly corporatization and equitization, will harden the budget constraint for SOEs and eliminate explicit and implicit government guarantees, thereby creating a more level playing

---

7. The level of nonperforming loans (NPLs) in Vietnam's banks is difficult to estimate because calculations are based on different accounting methods. In June 2003, the IMF estimated NPLs at $8–10 billion, which is equivalent to approximately 55–65 percent of total domestic credit. Only about $2 billion of this was thought to be recoverable. Standard & Poor's November estimate of the level of NPLs among Vietnam's state-owned banks is between 50 and 75 percent. In November, the State Bank governor said that the rate of overdue NPLs in Vietnam's joint stock banks had dropped from 14.0 percent to about 7.8 percent at the end of 2002, but that it could rise again in 2003 owing to bad loan decisions.

BOX 4.4
AGENCY FOR MANAGING STATE ASSETS:
MAIN PRINCIPLES OF OPERATION

Global experience illustrates the importance of insulating SOEs from misdirected bureaucratic and political influence so they can concentrate on maximizing shareholder value. State ownership rights need to be clearly distinguished from other economic rights (such as regulation). A single government agency that specializes in exercising state ownership rights would help separate the ownership function of the state from its other functions. It would also reduce the current fragmentation of authority and diffusion of responsibilities for SOEs. Several principles on how such agencies should operate have emerged from international experience:

• The ownership agency should be commercially focused and professional. Compensation for the agency's staff should be market based to attract staff with the necessary skills and expertise.

• The ownership agency's portfolio should include only for-profit, nonfinancial SOEs. Conflicts of interest will arise if nonfinancial and financial SOEs are relegated to the same agency. Furthermore, its attention will be diverted to maximizing shareholder value if nonprofits are included.

• The ownership agency's mandate should include both the management of state shares and, as appropriate, the sale of state shares (equity). When shares are sold, the agency should ultimately be responsible for the value of state shares and for the maximization of sale proceeds.

• State shareholder interests should be exercised through normal means, namely, annual shareholder meetings and SOE board appointments. This will give company management sufficient space to operate.

• The ownership agency should have broad authority with regard to its management and sale of shares. It should also have sole authority to vote the state's share at SOE annual shareholder meetings and to make SOE director appointments (proportional to the state's shareholding). This would be consistent with a nonpolitical and professional approach to the efficient use of capital.

• While seeking to maximize the efficient use of state capital, the ownership agency should implement financial management procedures that provide transparency and minimize risk.

SOURCE: Mako and Zhang (2002).

field with respect to access to financing. At present, state-owned enterprises continue to enjoy preferential access to financing, as is reflected in the large portion of credit going to them (50–60 percent of total lending by state-owned commercial banks) and in the high levels of nonperforming loans in the system. The growth of credit to the state-owned sector has continued to exceed the real growth rate of the economy even while the government has started reducing the number of SOEs (World Bank 2002: 10). The private sector, particularly its small and medium enterprises, are underserved by the banking sector.

Several factors on both the demand and the supply side of the credit market restrict private companies' access to bank financing. On the supply side, banks are reluctant to make loans to private enterprises because these firms do not enjoy the explicit or implicit guarantees associated with state ownership. As discussed in chapter 3, the factors that seem to influence private firms' access to bank financing are not important for SOEs, which suggests the two sectors have different regimes of access to bank lending. To level the playing field for access to bank loans, it will be necessary to harden the budget constraint on SOEs by removing the implicit or explicit backing of government agencies. Corporatization and equitization of non-strategic state-owned enterprises will be important steps toward leveling the playing field here. In the absence of implicit or explicit government guarantees, banks may be reluctant to lend to private companies because many of them lack the training and experience to conduct a good risk appraisal. With the recent removal of restrictions on interest rates, however, banks are now able to price the risk into their loans if they can assess it accurately. Hence banks need to strengthen their risk-assessment skills and develop the capacity to base their lending not only on collateral but also on the intrinsic merits of projects.

On the demand side, private enterprises are often reluctant to seek bank credit, because to qualify they must demonstrate higher levels of transparency in their business activities. According to the CIEM task force on the implementation of the Law on Enterprises, the majority of enterprises do not comply or fully comply with the financial reporting requirements of the Law. Only some 15–20 percent of enterprises prepare financial reports in accordance with Article 118 of the Law on Enterprises. Financial reports sent to business registration offices (to be publicized) are often cursory, inaccurate, and inadequate in form and substance (IFC 2003: 26).

Many private enterprises are forced to hide the true picture in order to avoid compliance with regulations that sometimes run against the nature and logic of normal business practices. Such regulations need to be amended, but policy changes will not be enough. Domestic private companies can and should take steps themselves to improve their access to credit and their ability to grow: some first steps would be to formalize their structures and operations, make their operations more transparent, and upgrade their management skills. Such measures would not only give Vietnam's private companies greater access to outside sources of finance but also increase their global competitiveness. But firms will make such moves only if they have confidence in the system and know that in doing so they will be rewarded with even greater political acceptance, less bureaucratic interference, and more access to finance.

Many of the newly emerging small and medium enterprises are in the services and information technology sectors, where intangible assets represent most of the balance sheet. These kinds of companies have special financing needs—mainly in the form of private equity and venture capital. Of the firms we surveyed, one-third of the private companies identified lack of access to outside equity as a major constraint. Aside from insurance companies, a leasing industry, and a fledgling stock market, Vietnam has few alternative forms of outside financing. For example, it has only seven venture capital/private equity firms with a staff of 30 or so professionals. The total capital under management is less than $200 million. In 2000 only $10 million of these funds went into new investments. To sustain the growth of private companies, especially in the services and hi-tech sectors, the development of alternative sources of financing has to be accelerated.

The general business environment for venture capital activities has improved markedly in the past three to four years, especially with the establishment of the stock market and the relaxation of restrictions on foreign investment in local private companies. Nevertheless, some obstacles remain, a primary one being the taxation regime for capital gains. Corporate income is taxed at relatively high rates, and punitive taxes are imposed on returns in excess of 20 percent. This system promotes opacity and makes it more difficult for venture capitalists to reach the level of comfort necessary for investment. In addition, concepts of corporate governance, particularly those pertaining to the protection of minority interests, are still in their infancy in Vietnam, and the development of the venture capital industry is especially sensitive to the degree of enforcement of property rights. Foreign venture capitalists face a number of restrictions as well regarding the business sectors in which they can invest and the ownership stakes allowed in domestic companies. Finally, the low level of development of the public equity market sets a limit to the extent to which venture capital can be a solution to funding problems at this stage.

Supporting Private Sector Growth through Market-Based Access to Land. As our survey showed, the main problem private firms face in accessing bank loans is insufficient collateral, which in turn stems largely from the difficulties with gaining access to land. Given the social costs of existing anomalies in the land administration system, reforms in this area should be a high priority, with the emphasis on shifting from a concessionary to a rights-based tenure system. One of the difficulties with the existing system is that despite constitutional and legal authority to transfer land-use rights, the state has to sanction all transactions. This power has been devolved to People's Committees at the provincial and district levels. Because administrative procedures are vague, there is ample room for bureaucratic discretion, which appears to be frequently exercised, for instance, to frustrate the distribution of land-use rights in bankruptcy. Unless the concessionary approach to land management changes, bureaucrats will continue to routinely disallow statutory rights to land. The shift toward a rights-based normative land-tenure system—although difficult, as it will affect entrenched bureaucratic interests—should be facilitated by the example of the Enterprise Law, which represents such a shift in the area of business registration.

In addition, the state should stop micromanaging private land transactions. It should not interfere with the negotiations between buyers and sellers and between borrowers and lenders within the general framework. The exchange of land-use rights should be structured mainly by the parties involved. Currently, the Land Department uses a standard form that is inflexible and makes it difficult to negotiate in order to meet the needs of particular lease transactions. Instead of putting a straitjacket on all private transactions, the government should provide and strengthen the legal framework for formulating and enforcing land-transfer contracts by establishing a registration authority, registration and revenue collection procedures, and penalties against illegal transactions.

Under the existing system of land administration, there are many delays in obtaining land-use rights and the cost of those rights is prohibitively high. Furthermore, domestic enterprises are responsible for compensation and resettlement in the leasing of recovered land from the government. Inasmuch as land is already allocated in Vietnam, any increase in specialized land has to come from other categories. To free the land for use, enterprises must pay twice: first for the land rental and second for vacancy of the land. This makes the value of the land-use rights very high. A more appropriate solution to the problem may be to make the state responsible in part for land compensation and clearance, with the costs to be included in the land rental.

To improve access to bank loans, it is essential that mortgages over land-use rights be enforced. This is as important as having these rights in the first place. Enforcement, however, remains problematic in Vietnam. The current law on secured transactions permits the mortgagor and the mortgagee to decide between themselves how to deal with the mortgaged land-use rights. This suggests that the land-use rights may be sold, assigned, or otherwise disposed of by the mortgagee following default. In practice, however, it is unclear whether a bank may sell or transfer the CLURs at its discretion. Government agencies have used this lack of clarity to interfere in the allocation of mortgaged land-use rights in cases of bankruptcy. In addition, certain regulatory provisions (such as Article 93 of Decree 24) seem to suggest that the purchaser of the mortgaged assets should continue the investment project (See Johnson, Stokes, and Master 2001). This places a further restriction on the value of such security and the use to which it can be put by lenders in achieving their primary aim, namely, the recovery of the loan proceeds advanced. At present, secured transactions in land need to be registered with the provincial Departments of Land and Housing or the People's Committees of subdistricts. No comprehensive, unified system of land registration detailing land use and land price tariffs is yet available to the public. This makes uncertainty regarding security arrangements all the greater.

The existing system of land administration discriminates between domestic and foreign users of land. This affects the ability of domestic enterprises to partner with foreign parties or to obtain financing from offshore financial institutions. Under the current land law, a private enterprise may contribute land-use rights to a joint venture only if the land rental has been paid for the entire term of the lease or there has been a prepayment of future land rentals for a period of at least five years (but not necessarily for the entire unexpired period of the lease). Since local businesses tend to be thinly capitalized, they find it difficult to pay the land rental for such long periods. Moreover, they have little in the way of cash and other assets to contribute. This limits their opportunities to cooperate with foreign investors and makes the investment environment less competitive. As a result, foreign investors are forced to cooperate more with state-owned enterprises, which are more strongly capitalized. The government should consider abolishing the restriction on private Vietnamese enterprises in contributing land-use rights to a joint venture, be it with a domestic or a foreign partner.

Investors often need to finance their investment projects in Vietnam by way of offshore loans. The current laws of Vietnam do not allow domestic enterprises to grant a mortgage of land-use rights to an offshore lender to secure the repayment of the loan. This in effect prevents domestic enterprises from borrowing in the long term from offshore financial institutions. Currently, foreign-invested enterprises are unable to rent land directly from nongovernment entities. This creates an incentive to adopt suboptimal contractual arrangements and encourages informality. Regulations should be amended to enable foreign-invested enterprises to lease land from private enterprises, individuals, and households.

The current legal and regulatory framework also creates disincentives for converting land from personal to firm ownership. The tenure regimes of residential and commercial land are very different. Land used for residential purposes is granted by the government at no cost. Land used for commercial purposes cannot be granted but has to be leased from the government. The transformation of residential land to commercial land entails significant costs for the household. To begin with, it has to pay a registration fee equal up to 20 percent of the value of the land-use rights. Then the household business must pay annual rentals and, most important, must trade effective long-term ownership for a renewable five-year leasehold. Furthermore, the lease must be prepaid for at least five years in order for the land to be available as collateral. Residential property can be used for the same purposes without incurring any of these costs.

Under this land regime, household enterprises are reluctant to convert to formal private enterprises. This constrains the growth of already established small and medium enterprises into larger ones. By remaining in this category, however, household enterprises are subject to other restrictions. For example, they cannot export directly. The different legal regimes for residential and commercial land also create an uneven playing field in certain sectors: hotels built on residential land, for example, can compete against hotels built on commercial land. The transaction costs associated with converting land from residential to commercial use should be reduced so that enterprises can adopt the legal form that is most suitable for their growth plans and strategy. At present, undercapitalized private firms are unwilling or unable to borrow from banks because they do not convert property from residential to commercial classification in order to avoid having to pay land rentals.

Conclusion

Private sector growth is key to maintaining vigorous growth in Vietnam and achieving its development objectives. Above all, private enterprises need space to grow. Regulations that run counter to the logic of normal market practices, that limit the opportunities for entrepreneurs to enter into contractual relationships, or that penalize them for market success are bound to be circumvented, at significant social costs. By contrast, laws and regulations that are in line with market forces will be easier to implement, and their implementation will be supported by the same market forces they intend to protect. Adapting laws and regulations to the needs of the marketplace will not be enough, however. Incentives within the bureaucracy need to be aligned with development. A bureaucracy that is committed to development will find it beneficial to support the growth of the private sector.

References

Andreoni, James, Brian Erard, and Jonathan Feinstein. 1998. "Tax Compliance." *Journal of Economic Literature* 36(2): 818–60.

AusAID. 2000. "Vietnam: Land Administration." Working Paper 4. Canberra, Australia.

Bai, Chong-En, David D. Li, Yingyi Qian, and Yijiang Wang. 1999. "Anonymous Banking and Financial Repression: How Does China's Reform Limit Government Predation without Reducing Its Revenue?" Stanford University Working Paper. Available at http://www-econ.stanford.edu/faculty/workp/swp99014.pdf.

Batra, Geeta, Daniel Kaufmann, and Andrew Stone. 2002. *Voices of the Firms: Investment Climate and Governance Findings of the World Business Environment Survey (WBES)*. World Bank.

Belser, Patrick. 2000. "Vietnam: On the Road to Labor-Intensive Growth?" Background Paper for the Vietnam Development Report 2000. Washington, D.C.: World Bank.

Belser, Patrick, and Martin Rama. 2002. "State Ownership and Labor Redundancy: Estimates Based on Enterprise-Level Data from Vietnam." World Bank Working Paper 2599. Washington, D.C.

Botero, Juan, Simeon Djankov, Rafael La Porta, Florencio López-de-Silanes, and Andrei Shleifer. 2002. "The Regulation of Labor." World Bank Draft Paper. Washington, D.C. Available at http://rru.worldbank.org/DoingBusiness/TopicReports/LaborRegulations.aspx.

Cao Minh Truc. 2002. "Some Measures to Boost Domestic Investment." Paper presented at the Vietnam Business Forum, Hanoi, December 9.

Central Institute of Economic Management (CIEM). 2000. *Vietnam's Economy in 1999*. Hanoi.

———. 2002. The Enterprise Law's Enforcement: Achievements, Challenges and Solutions. Hanoi.

———. 2003. Assessment Report on Three Years of the Implementation of the Law of Enterprises. Hanoi.

Chan, Vincent. 2002. *Private Sector in China.* UBS Warburg.

Coolidge, Jacqueline. 2003. "International Benchmarks for Administrative Barriers and Lessons Concerning Reforms." South Asia FDI Roundtable. Maldives: FIAS.

Dinh Duc Sinh. 2002. "Some Matters on Land and the Promotion of the Development of a Multi-sectoral Economy." Paper presented at the Hanoi Association of Industry and Commerce conference, Land for Production and Business: Current Status and Solutions, November.

Djankov, Simeon, Rafael La Porta, Florencio López-De-Silanes, and Andrei Shleifer. 2002. "The Regulation of Entry." *Quarterly Journal of Economics* 117 (1): 1–37.

Do Dinh Luong, Nguyen Thi Thanh Hang, Stefan Nijwening, and Ramon Hagad. 2002. *Evaluation of One Stop Shops in Vietnam.* Swiss Agency for Development and Cooperation and Government Committee for Organisation and Personnel of Vietnam. Hanoi, Vietnam.

Dollar, David. 2002. "Reform, Poverty and Growth in Vietnam." Policy Research Working Paper 2837. World Bank, Washington, D.C.

Friedman, Eric, Simon Johnson, Daniel Kaufmann, and Pablo Zoido Lobaton. 2000. "Dodging the Grabbing Hand: The Determinants of Unofficial Activity in 69 Countries." *Journal of Public Economics* 76: 459–93.

General Statistical Office of Vietnam. 2001. "Some Issues in Compilation of Main Accounts by Institutional Sectors in Vietnam." Country Report for Interregional Workshop on the 1993 System of National Accounts, May 7–11, Manila, Philippines.

Government of Vietnam. 2001. *Report on Comprehensive Needs Assessment for the Development of Vietnam's Legal System for Period 2001–2010.* Hanoi.

Gregory, Neil, Stoyan Tenev, and Dileep Wagle. 2000. *China's Emerging Private Enterprises.* Washington, D.C.: International Finance Corporation.

Ha, K. Oanh. 2003. "Taking Stocks to the Street: Vietnam's Unofficial Stock Market Is Booming." *Mercury News.* Available at www.bayarea.com/mld/mercurynews/business/4959959.htm.

Institute of Law Research. 1999. *The Social Research on Household and Land-Use Rights in Hanoi City in 1998*. Hanoi: Ministry of Justice.

International Finance Corporation (IFC), World Bank, and Mekong Project Development Facility (MPDF). 2003. "Vietnam Business Forum." Midyear Consultative Group Meeting. Hanoi: World Bank Group.

International Monetary Fund (IMF). 2001. *Vietnam, Selected Issues and Statistical Appendix*. Washington, D.C.

———. 2002a. Vietnam: Selected Issues and Statistical Appendix. Washington, D.C.

———. 2002b. International Financial Statistics.

JBIC. 2002. *Survey of Vietnamese Enterprises*. Hanoi.

Jin, Hehui, and Yingyi Qian. 1998. "Public vs. Private Ownership of Firms: Evidence from Rural China." *Quarterly Journal of Economics* 113 (3): 773–808.

Johnson, Stokes, and Master. 2001. "Land Issues." Discussion paper presented at Vietnam Business Forum, Hanoi.

Litvack, Jennie, and Dennis Rondinelli. 1999. *Market Reform in Vietnam: Building Institutions for Development*. Westport, Conn.: Quorum.

Loyaza, Norman. 1996. *The Economics of the Informal Sector: A Simple Model and Some Empirical Guidance from Latin America*. Carnegie Rochester Conference Series on Public Policy: 45: 126–62.

Mako, William, and Chunlin Zhang. 2002. "Exercising Ownership Rights in State-Owned Enterprise Groups: What China Can Learn from International Experience." World Bank, Beijing. Mimeo.

McMillan, John, and Christopher Woodruff. 1998. "Networks, Trust, and Search in Vietnam's Emerging Private Sector." Social Science Research Network. Available at http://www.ssrn.com.

———. 2002. "The Central Role of Entrepreneurs in Transition Economies." *Journal of Economic Perspectives* 16 (3): 153–70.

Morisset, Jacques, and Olivier Lumenga Neso. 2002. "Administrative Barriers to Foreign Investment in Developing Countries." Working Paper. Washington, D.C.: FIAS. Available at http://econ.worldbank.org/files/15291_wps2848.pdf.

Naughton, Barry. 1995. *Growing Out of the Plan*. New York: Cambridge University Press.

Nguyen Dinh Tai. 2002. "Some Issues in Obtaining Land-Use Rights for Production and Business by the Private Sector." Paper presented at the Hanoi Association of Industry and Commerce conference, Land for Production and Business: Current Status and Solutions, November.

Nguyen Phuong Quynh Trang and Jonathan R. Stromseth. 2002. *Business Associations in Vietnam: Status, Role and Performance.* Hanoi: Mekong Project Development Facility.

Olson, Mancur Jr. 1982. *The Rise and Decline of Nations.* New Haven, Conn.: Yale University Press.

Oxford Analytica. 2002. "Vietnam: China Offers Model for State Corporate Reform." October 30.

Phan The D. 2001. "A Sectoral Analysis of Income Under-reporting in Vietnam." Paper prepared for the 30th Annual Conference of Economists, University of Western Australia, September 23–26.

Portes, Alejandro, Manuel Castells, and Lauren Benton. 1989. "World Underneath: The Origins, Dynamics, and Effects of the Infomal Economy." In A. Portes, M. Castells, and L. Benton, eds., *The Informal Economy: Studies in Advanced and Less Developed Countries.* Baltimore, Md.: Johns Hopkins.

Qian, Yingyi. 2001. *How Reform Worked in China.* University of California at Berkeley. http://llsa.Berkeley.edu/~yqian/research.html.

Quinn, Brian J. M. 2002. "Legal Reform and Its Context in Vietnam." *Columbia Journal of Asian Law* (Spring): 221-91.

Rapaczynski, Andrzej. 1996. "The Role of State and the Market in Establishing Property Rights." *Journal of Economic Perspectives* 10 (Spring): 87–103.

Schneider, Friedrich. 2002. "Size and Measurement of the Informal Economy in 110 Countries around the World." Paper presented at a Workshop of the Australian National Tax Centre.

Schneider, Friedrich, and Dominik Enste. 2000. "Shadow Economies: Size, Causes, and Consequences." *Journal of Economic Literature* 38: 77–114.

Tenev, Stoyan, and Chunlin Zhang. 2002. "Corporate Governance and Enterprise Reform in China: Building the Institutions of Modern Markets." Washington, D.C.: International Finance Corporation.

Thanh Nguyen, 2002. "Impact of the Current Tax System on the Business Environment." Paper presented at the Vietnam Business Forum, Hanoi, December 9.

Tokman, Victor. 1992. "The Informal Sector in Latin America: From Underground to Legal." In V. Tokman, ed., *Beyond Regulation: The Informal Economy in Latin America*. Boulder, CO: PREALC, Lynne Rienner.

Tran Phuong Binh. 2002. "Remarks by Ho Chi Minh Youth Business Association." Paper presented at the Vietnam Business Forum, Hanoi, December 9.

Vietnam Business Forum, various issues.

Vietnam Chamber of Commerce and Industry (VCCI). 2000. *Survey Report on the Implementation of the Enterprise Law, Impediments to and Recommendations for the Development of Private Sector.* Hanoi.

Vietnam Country Commercial Guide FY2002. 2002. U.S. Department of Commerce. http://www.ustrade.gov/website/ccg.nsf/CCGurl/CCG-Vietnam2002.

Webster, Leila. 1999. "SMEs in Vietnam: On the Road to Prosperity." Private Sector Discussion Series. Hanoi: Mekong Private Sector Development Facility.

Webster, Leila, and Markus Taussig. 1999. *Vietnam's Undersized Engine: A Survey of 95 Larger Private Manufacturers*. Hanoi: Mekong Private Sector Development Facility.

World Bank. 2000. *Public Expenditures Review*. Hanoi.

———. 2001. *Vietnam 2010: Entering the 21st Century*. Vietnam Development Report. Hanoi.

———. 2002. *Implementing Reforms for Faster Growth and Poverty Reduction*. Vietnam Development Report. Hanoi.

Yao, Yang. 2000. "Government Commitment and the Outcome of Privatization in China." Beijing University, mimeo. http://www.nber.org/~confer/2001/ease/yao.pdf.

About the Authors

Stoyan Tenev is lead economist in the East Asia and Pacific Department at the International Finance Corporation; Amanda Carlier is senior private sector development specialist at the World Bank in Hanoi, Vietnam; Omar Chaudry is an economist with the East Asia and Pacific Department at the International Finance Corporation; and Quynh-Trang Nguyen is business development officer with the Mekong Private Sector Development Facility in Hanoi.